When ~~sh~~I.T.Happens...

the business owner's bible to Scams, Viruses and the other vagaries of battling day to day IT issues...

By Chris Blunt

Entrepreneur, IT Guru and Head of Making things work at one of the UKs most loved I.T. Companies...

Copyright

When shI.T. Happens: *The business owner's bible to Scams, Viruses and the other vagaries of battling day to day IT issues...*

Copyright © 2014 by Chris Blunt
All rights reserved. This book or any portion thereof
may not be reproduced or used in any manner whatsoever
without the express written permission of the publisher
except for the use of brief quotations in a book review.

First Printing, 2014
ISBN-13: 978-1499178739
ISBN-10: 1499178735

Published by B.S Net Limited T/A brokenStones, providers of I.T. Support & Consultancy to UK based Businesses - www.brokenstones.co.uk

Bridge House, Station Road, Lichfield, WS13 6HX
+44 (0) 1543 241016
http://chrisbluntbooks.co.uk

If you like this book…

Based on the fantastic feedback I get about the weekly E-mails that this book is based on, I'm confident you'll find this something of enormous use. I'd encourage you to be ruthless with this book, scribble all over and rip pages out when you find something useful. Don't be afraid!

If you like this book I'd be grateful if you'd post some positive feedback on Amazon or other book review sites, and of course feel free to share any comments on Facebook & twitter too.

You can also signup to the weekly mailing list that was the inspiration for the content in this book at http://chrisbluntbooks.co.uk/toptips/

I'd love to hear any feedback via http://facebook.com/brokenStonesIT or Twitter: @brokenstones

Acknowledgements

I'd like to thank all the readers of my weekly emails and all the fantastic feedback they've provided over the last year. I'm really passionate about seeing I.T. done properly, and making sure I.T. works for you, it's been amazing to see how my tips have helped so many.

An extra special mention to all those who have sent in specific questions that have provided ideas and content for these e-mails.

About the Author

Chris Blunt is owner and 'Head of Making things work' at brokenStones an I.T. support and Consultancy business in Lichfield, Staffordshire. Chris set the business up back in 2006 from a desire to make a difference to small businesses by providing IT services that are professional, dependable and cost effective.

His Key Technical Skills include Email Systems, Domains, Network Security and 'doing whatever it takes' to really get IT working for small businesses.

Graduating from Lancaster University in 2001 with a BSc Hons in Computer Science, Chris began his Professional IT career as a Software Programmer before seeing the opportunity to turn his hobby into a career and stepped into an IT Management role. It was during this time Chris started to develop his vision for brokenStones. Travelling all over the UK he saw many small businesses up-close and witnessed the poor level of IT services they were getting.

During his career Chris has worked for some of the world's largest organisations, such as Yahoo! along with some of the smallest one man bands... but his passion lies in helping owners of small and medium sized businesses *really* get their I.T. working for them.

To sum Chris up, he is one of the nicest guys you will ever meet, he is a true IT expert in every sense and he makes IT work for your business.

Chris is usually accompanied by his trusty Border Collie, Donald, who is the most excitable and loveable dog you could ever hope to meet.

12 months of fun, serious and damn useful emails…PLUS a couple of extras on me…

Subject: **Introduction** 10
Subject: **Should I pay the Ransom?** 13
Subject: **What would you do?** 14
Subject: **Are you OK?** 16
Subject: **Your recent order** 19
Subject: **Who's using your password?** 21
Subject: **I feel a bit of an idiot this week…** 25
Subject: **Did you get my E-Mail?** 27
Subject: **Can you change your password please?** 32
Subject: **I've noticed there is a problem with your computer.** ... 35
Subject: **Who else is using your password?** 37
Subject: **The most useful program on my computer.** 39
Subject: **Have you got a 'lifebuoy' for your business?** 43
Subject: **Did you get the job?** 45
Subject: **It's all I seem to be talking about at the moment.** 47
Subject: **It made me blush…** 49
Subject: **What does your E-Mail address say about you?** 52
Subject: **Who is reading your E-Mails?** 54
Subject: **Really Sorry, but I've managed to double book** 55
Subject: **Missing E-Mail** 57
Subject: **The 2nd most useful program on my computer** 60
Subject: **Just what does that mean?** 63
Subject: **I thought we had a meeting?** 65
Subject: **What do you mean it's not backed up?** 68

Subject: **I think there is a problem with your website?** 71
Subject: **Just checking you got the attachment?** 76
Subject: **Really, what's the point of E-Mail signatures?** 79
Subject: **What next...** 82
Subject: **Unbelievable Photo** 85
Subject: **It's just a copy... a good one, but still just a copy...** 87
Subject: **The Easiest way to remember your password** 89
Subject: **Are you going to fix it, or just ignore it?** 91
Subject: **Isn't that *your* domain name?** 95
Subject: **Conned Again** 99
Subject: **I'm just trying to get home** 101
Subject: **Please see the attached** 105
Subject: **Are you online?** 108
Subject: **What is the problem?** 112
Subject: **Simples** 116
Subject: **I thought you were away?** 119
Subject: **One of the hidden costs in business** 124
Subject: **Why is it some people can just do things quicker?** 126
Subject: **Don't jump off the bed!** 128
Subject: **What's Up?** 130
Subject: **Can I get rid of all these cables?** 132
Subject: **Is this really what you want to read today?** 134
Subject: **Reminder: Put the Bins Out** 135
Subject: **Time for a change?** 137
Subject: **Can you use a different browser please?** 138
Subject: **How did you do that?** 141
Subject: **Just forget about it** 144
Subject: **I just can't do without two...** 146

Subject: **Are you happy to risk EVERYTHING?** 148
Subject: **An Intriguing Offer** 150
Subject: **Want to know more?** 151
Subject: **The Giveaways** 152

Disclaimer

PLEASE NOTE: What you are about to read may cause you to question or worry about your own I.T. systems. I strongly urge you, if you have any concerns at all, to speak to your Local Trusted I.T. provider.

The following e-mails are designed to help you make better use of, and stay safe when using your computer. If you are at all unsure please ask an expert for advice, I make no warranties or accept any responsibility or liability for any adverse effects from following any of the advice in this book.

We rely on our I.T. Systems to run our businesses. When they break or go wrong it can cause us major problems. Don't leave these things to chance.

If you are at all unsure, don't have anyone to call, or you don't get an answer that you feel comfortable with then please,

Feel free to call my helpdesk on 01543 241 016.

We are available during normal UK business hours and are always eager to help. We will be able to give you quick and simple advice over the phone. If you need more in depth work doing will happily provide you with a list of services to suit your needs.

As Thomas Jefferson said,

"The Price of Freedom is eternal vigilance"

From: Chris Blunt chrisblunt@brokenstones.co.uk
Sent: 17th April 2014
Subject: **Introduction**

Hi,

Thanks for picking up my book, on the following pages I'll share with you 12 months of fun, serious and damn useful emails sent to savvy business owners who simply want their computers to work.

The emails were sent every single week (yes, even over Christmas - get's me out the house!) to members of an IT club to help side-step viruses, recognise those dodgy scam emails and keep business computers running like a dream.

They were written by me, a dog loving, computer loving, family loving guy from Lichfield who helps hundreds of business owners love their computers (again).

This book is 100% non-geeky and non-technical. It's just packed with golden, easy to understand I.T. tips that GUARANTEE business computers help your business rather than hinder it.

The emails are collectively a blueprint for IT peace-of-mind for any business owner with a computer (that they sometimes want to throw out of the window – we've all been there!). Real life stories and feedback are all included to show the perils and delights of modern technology.

I've had so much great feedback over the last year from my I.T. Club members that it felt like a disservice to you if I didn't put the entire collection together in a book to share with everyone else.

This is my 12 month email diary.

This is as they got sent out. This is NOT the abridged version.

This is my advice.

I hope you enjoy, learn and remember a "Computer is for life, not just for Christmas"

Chris Blunt & Donald (the dog)

Top Tip:

Whenever you find a really useful tip, rip the page out... don't be afraid, I'm not going to come round and check to see if my book is still intact on your bookshelf, I'd be far prouder to see it being put to good use!

Rip the page out, scribble all over it and stick it up on your wall. If you are really precious and want a 'mint condition copy' drop me an email with a photo of what you've done to your current copy and I might just send you a signed version!

From: Chris Blunt chrisblunt@busstopgroup.co.uk

Sent: 20th February

Subject: **Should I pay the Ransom?**

I've seen this a few times now, but what I hadn't realised was **some people do actually take it seriously!**

We had someone use our drop off and diagnose service the other week, "My Computers not working properly" was the message they left us with...

On starting it up, it was clear it was infected with a particularly nasty virus, it's the one that fills the screen with a **'Police'** message saying something along the lines of "**Your computer has been locked due to the detection of illegal activity**".

We have seen a variety of these along the same theme now, some we've been able to clean up, some we've ended up having to rebuild the whole computer.

But this was the first time I'd actually had someone ask me **"What's the cost if we pay the fine?"** Well I have to say I was flabbergasted, I thought it was blatantly obvious this was a scam, but they really thought it was real (*No I didn't ask what they'd been looking at!!!*)

Top Tip

Before you put ANY payment (or other personal details) in to your computer, think about it very carefully, did you ask for this, could it be a scam?

From: Chris Blunt chrisblunt@busstopgroup.co.uk

Sent: 27th February

Subject: **What would you do?**

If you'd just placed an order on Amazon and then you got the email below through a few hours later, **what would you think?**

> From: Amazon [mailto:infos@amazon.co.uk]
> Sent: 03 February 2013 02:55
> Subject: Notification
>
> We want to inform you that your account was accessed from an unauthorized computer.
>
> Please visit https://www.amazon.co.uk and confirm that you are the owner of the account.
>
> Login
> https://www.amazon.co.uk

What do you think? Would you be **tempted to click the link**?

What made this even more tempting was the recipient of this e-mail had just placed on order via their iPad for the first time...

Luckily they had the good sense to send it over to us before doing anything with it and we were able to advise them **it's a scam**.

There are a few ways to tell (Firstly I'm not aware of Amazon sending this type of thing out anyway!) but usually the most obvious and easiest is to **hover over the link** (DON'T CLICK!) and see what it actually shows...

> Please visit https://www.amazon.co.uk and confirm that you
>
> Login :
> https://www.amazon.co.uk
>
> http://mail.aronfeld.com/uk/
> Click to follow link

Can you see **it's not actually got anything to do with Amazon!** (aronfel.com)
It may have just been a coincidence and good timing (There are a lot of these emails being sent out!) but it's still worth **changing your password** and running a virus and malware scan on your computer just in case...

Top Tip:

Treat any email asking you to 'Login to confirm your account details" with suspicion, most major players will never send you an email asking you to login to confirm details. Always hover over the link before clicking to check it out, better still rather than click the email link, open up Google and search for the site instead... I always do this with my banking. Always.

15

```
From: Chris Blunt chrisblunt@busstopgroup.co.uk
Sent: 7th March
Subject: Are you OK?
```

I'm sure you'll have seen a scam like this before, these e-mails have been going round for some time now, in various forms, but the gist of them is usually the same.

Someone you know (well you are in their contact address book at least), is abroad, they've been attacked and had all their money, cards, phones stolen and now they need some money to get home.

They are asking you for help.

> Hello
>
> This message is coming to you with great depression due to my state of discomfort. I came down here to Madrid Spain with my family for a short vacation but unfortunately, we were mugged and robbed at the park of the hotel where we stayed. All cash, credit cards and cell phones were stolen off us but we still have our lives and passports.
>
> We've been to the embassy and the police here and they have done the best they can. Our flight leaves in few Hrs from now but we are having problems settling the hotel bills and the hotel manager won't let us leave until we settle the bills which is $1,950. I am contacting you to ask for a short loan which I will refund immediately I get my family back home safely. Let me know if you can help.
>
> Looking forward to positive response.

The way this works has changed a bit over the years, but the general format now is…

1.   Scammer hacks in to persons e-mail account (usually from a weak password)
2.   Scammer sends email to most people in personal address book
3.   Anyone that responds the scammer then replies back to

from a **different** email account (usually with 1 letter different in the email address, so you don't really notice)
4.   Email conversation will continue and ask for a money transfer via Western Union

So what can you do about this?
Well first it goes without saying if you receive any email like this, or asking for anything out of the ordinary, treat it
with **extreme** suspicion, these e-mails prey on good nature and kindness.

Is there anything you can do to stop your own email account being hacked?
This scam all hinges on access to your email account in the first place, and that is usually down to a simple password or using the same password across multiple websites?

- Is your password your pets name?

- Or your own name, perhaps with a number on the end?

- Is your email password the same as your facebook, ebay and LinkedIn passwords?

You'll have seen in the news of high profile sites being hacked and peoples account details being stolen, the trouble when you use the same password across several sites is if one gets hacked and your email address and password stolen, the first thing they do is try that password on your email account!

I wrote a guide some time ago on tips for creating secure passwords, let me know if you'd like a copy and I'll dig it out for you,

It's also worth noting, that although it does not prevent it, it does make it a bit more difficult for the scammer if you don't have a 'public' email account (like yahoo or Hotmail), it's a bit more difficult for them to work out how and where to access your email if you are not on a widely known email provider (let me know if you'd like more info on this too.)

> **Top Tip:**
>
> Don't use easy to guess passwords, like the names of your family, pets, or simple words. For logins you use a lot (like your email, facebook etc), use different passwords on each one. I have various 'levels' of passwords that I use, depending how often I use them and how important they are.

From: Chris Blunt chrisblunt@busstopgroup.co.uk

Sent: 14th March

Subject: **Your recent order**

I've had a number of people email me over the last couple of weeks with this one, it's proving quite popular at the moment,

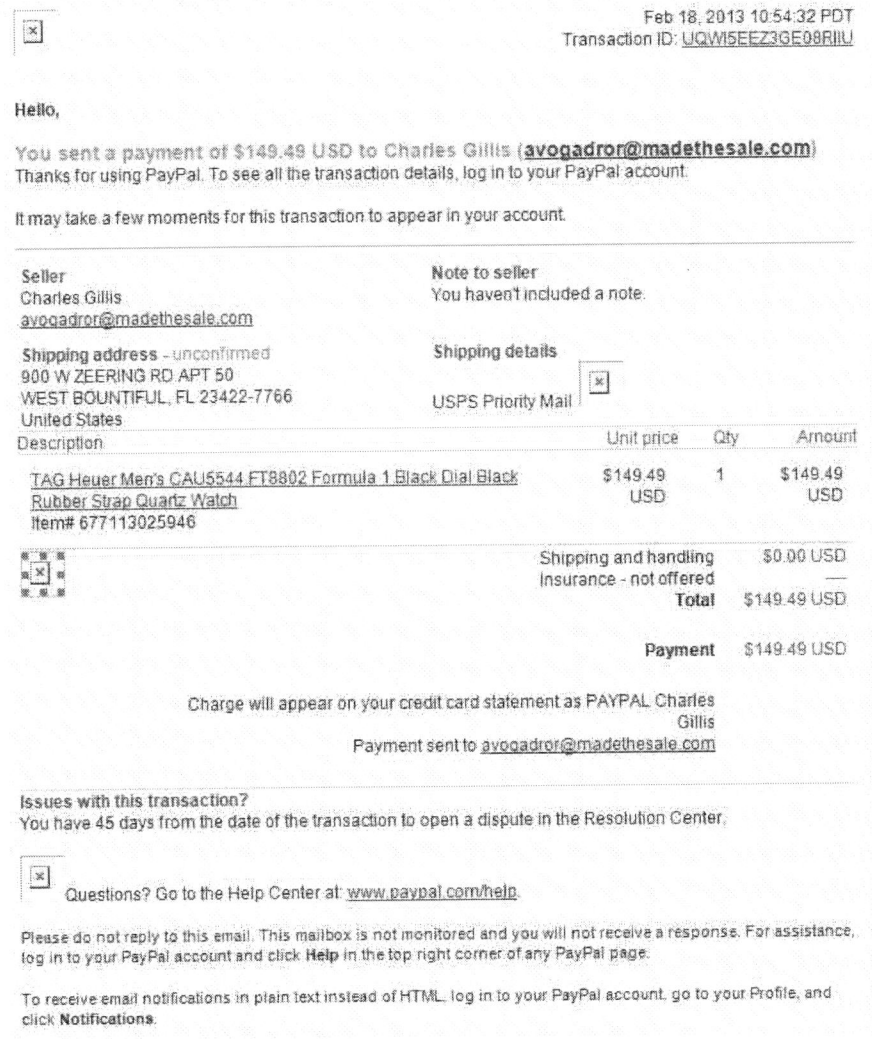

These are designed to scare you in to thinking someone has just

hacked your eBay or Paypal account and bought something, when in actual fact they are hoping to panic you in to clicking the link. Remember you can hover over the link (Don't Click!) to see where it will take you, see what happens when I hover over the 'www.paypal.com/help' link here:

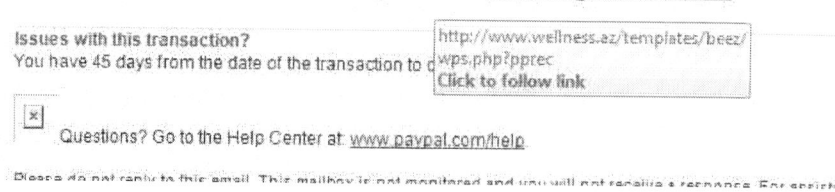

It's actually got nothing to with PayPal has it? This will end up taking you to a site that 'looks' like Paypal in the hope that you will panic and put in your login details. They will then use these to actually login and use your account! Make Sense?

There are hundreds of thousands of these e-mails going out everyday, it costs them very, very little to do, and they only need a minuscule amount of people to click and take action to make it worth their while. Don't be one of their victims!

If you think you may have recently fallen for one of these, the first thing you should do is change your password (Remember what I said about searching for the REAL site on Google rather than using an email link!), and if you're still worried give us a call.

Top Tip:

As I said a few weeks ago, if you are at all unsure, the best thing to do is to go to Google and 'search' for Paypal, login this way and check your account. Never click the links in emails like this, or any email you are remotely unsure about.

```
From: Chris Blunt chrisblunt@busstopgroup.co.uk
Sent: 21st March
Subject: Who's using your password?
```

In response to a number of conversations I've had lately about passwords, and how to remember them, I thought it might help to share with you some of the tips and techniques I've come across over the years. I've created a PDF guide for you to download if you want something to keep as a reference - Chris's Tip's for creating a memorable Password

I'm not going to get in to a discussion on why you should use a secure password and why you should not use the same password across everything that you do, I happily discuss that with you another time if you wish?

If I can just give you a few tips and tricks to creating more secure passwords, and some easy ways to remember them then hopefully that should be of some use for you today.

I forgot my password!
Don't worry about forgetting a password, it's better than having an easy to guess one! Remember **most passwords can be easily reset** either by simply clicking an 'I forgot my password' link or by calling your relevant IT provider <cough, cough> who should be able to reset the password to any system **they** look after for you (despite some myths, we don't have access to EVERY system you use...).

I do have some systems which only require the password when I first set them up on my phone or my computer, so I deliberately set a really long, random password that I use once, and then if I ever need it again, I simply reset it, I just find it easier that way, and it's one less thing to remember!

Is it just password?
A quick look at what's NOT a good password...

password (Yes I know some people that just use 'password', for some quite secure stuff too!)

> ### Giveaway #1 – Free Password Guide
> You can go and grab my free guide to creating memorable passwords by visiting: http://chrisbluntbooks.co.uk/freepasswordguide/

Chrisb1 (Using your name, even with a few numbers tagged on the end is not a smart move)

Donald051207 (Pet's name with their date of birth - I'd have used my daughters but I find Donald's easier to remember ;))

In truth any 'plain' password is not a great move, they are easy to figure out, either by guessing based on personal information or using a 'dictionary attack' (a long list of words or phrases that they keep trying till one works).

I've also found **a lot of people think they can only use letters or numbers in their password**, but take a look at your keyboard... most of the symbols you see can be used, and don't forget it's not an English lesson, you don't have to use a capital only at the start of a word!

Obviously by far the best password is a long series of random characters that use a mix of letters (both upper and lowercase, numbers and symbols) but if I asked you to remember this, could you?

T8mch7r,t@ratf\/\/,$c0t7wA(k

Passwords are like underwear, Don't leave yours lying around...
The truth is very few of us have the gifted ability to remember a random sequence, so short of writing it down, we need a few techniques to help us make the sequence 'appear' random. Please feel free to use any of them, or a combination of all of them!

Memorable Words and numbers
The least secure of the three, it involves picking a memorable word or number that you find easy to remember, but is not connected to you in anyway, for example, you like to read the paper in the morning, and happen know the empire state building has 102 storey's so you come up with news102paper, and then you decide to spell it wrong, perhaps knews!02Papier – Notice how I've added the extra k at the start, held down the 'SHIFT' key when typing the 1 and P and added an 'i' in to paper?

Cryptic Words
These can work well with the memorable words and involves replacing certain characters in a word with numbers or symbols, for instance an 'a' could become an '@' or an 'S' could turn in to '5' or even 'E' in to '£' (Remember what I said about the pound symbol above?

c@n-U-R3@D-thi$?

Passphrases

23

Finally, passphrases are my favourite, I find them a great way of creating really random sequences that are easy to remember.

Start by thinking of a memorable phrase "Go and wash your mouth out with soap and water"

Now by taking the first letter of each word we can form a new shorter phrase

Gawymowsaw

Now sprinkle in a few of the cryptic words technique

g@Wym0w$Aw

What do you think? Personally I find using an upper case after a symbol flows quite well when typing and is easier to remember.

Don't worry - if this all seems a bit much, go and grab my PDF guide have a read of that which gives some more examples, try a few out yourself and if you're still struggling give me a call, or come along to our next IT Clinic

Top Tip:

Use passwords that don't mean anything to you, the less of a link there is to yourself, the harder it is for someone to guess it!

Make sure you have a good mix of letters, numbers and symbols, it makes it much, much harder for automated systems to 'crack' your password.

Remember most passwords can be reset quite easily, the most annoying one I have is for an account I use once every 3 months, I can never remember it and always have to send off a signed form to ask them to reset it, it takes about 20 minutes.

```
From: Chris Blunt chrisblunt@busstopgroup.co.uk
Sent: 27th March
```
Subject: **I feel a bit of an idiot this week...**

Slightly embarrassing this week, after all the details I've sent you on scam emails lately, I got this one through myself last week...

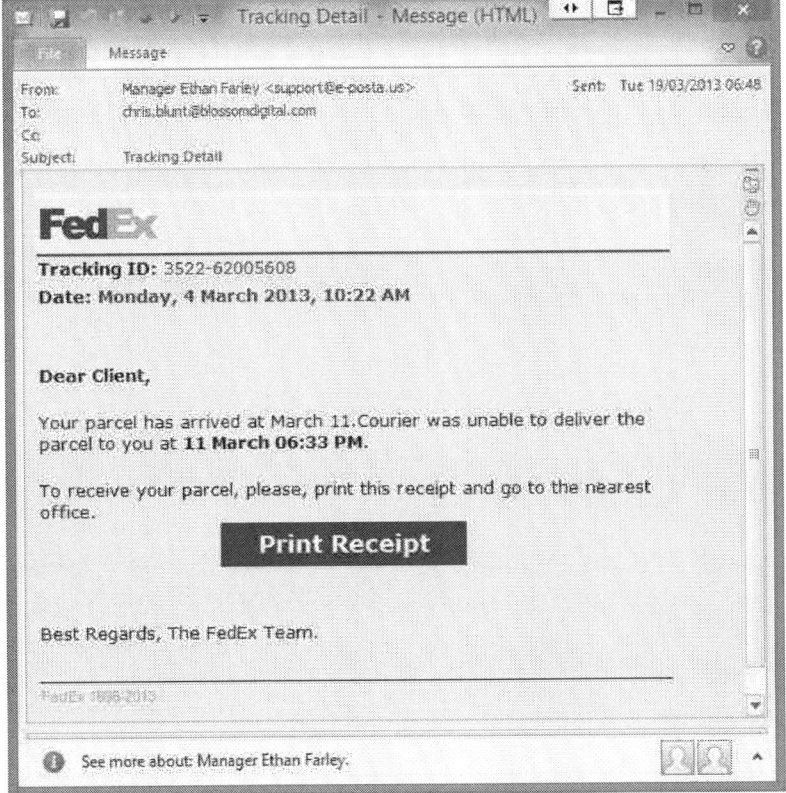

Having recently sent a parcel to a client in the US, by FedEx, I saw it and thought "Excellent, it's got there" and forwarded it over to Rachael to let her know she could tick it off.

It was only when she phoned me to say what do you want me to do with this that I realised I'd been suckered!

You see she read it properly and noticed it said "Unable to deliver", that's when I took another look and realised it's another scam email...

And yes (between me and you), it did make me feel like a bit of an idiot!

On closer inspection there are a few things wrong here:
- The Dates - Why is the email sent on the 19th, dated the 4th and talking about a parcel on the 11th?
- "Deliver to you" – If I'd read it properly I'd have been a bit more suspect!
- The 'Print Receipt' Link is not right (How many times have I said to check that recently!)
- The E-mail address it's been sent to is a really old one I don't use any more
- (and this is where I really should have known better!) I didn't actually have anything to do with sending the parcel; someone else in my office did, so why would I be getting an email?

In my defence I would say, had I been inclined to click the 'Print Receipt' button, I would have checked the link first, that's just habit for me. I'd encourage you to do the same, even in emails from people you trust – it's easy for their email to be hacked, or for a virus to infect their machine and send malicious email out...

Top Tip:

Make a habit of checking every link you click, it only takes a second to pause over a link before you click it.

```
From: Chris Blunt chrisblunt@busstopgroup.co.uk
Sent: 4th April
Subject: Did you get my E-Mail?
```

I'm not sure if you caught the Chris Evans show on Radio Two last week, but he posed the question...

"You know when you send an email, and you get the tick in the box to say its sent successfully, but it doesn't get there... where does it go to?"

I'm not going to go in to the technical why's and wherefores' of what happens to E-mail when you hit send, if it's at that stage, you should really speak to an E-Mail expert (it just so happens you can reach a couple on 01543 241 016 – ask for the E-Mail commandos!).

I will warn you, E-mail is my specialist subject, I've tried to be as concise as I can for you, and if you do make it all the way to the end I've shared a little secret with you, it's a simple, sure fire way to guarantee your e-mail got to where it was supposed to...

Firstly we need to dispel a couple of myths that some people don't realise...

Myth #1

E-Mail is NOT a guaranteed delivery method – It's the same as sending something first class post, it usually gets there, not always, and of course there is no guarantee anyone will actually read it (or that it got to the right person!)

Myth #2

E-Mail is NOT an instantaneously delivery, just because email usually gets there within a minute or two, doesn't always mean it will, there are a number of deliberate (and non-deliberate) things that can happen to delay email.

The Top Three Reasons E-Mail doesn't get to where it's going...

1. Believe it or not, **The most common reason** we come across for why **e-mail doesn't get to where it's supposed too** - it's got the wrong address on it...

2. The **Second most common reason.....** – it does!! it's just the other person has not read it, or they've deleted it, or just ignored it...

3. The **3rd most common reason** email doesn't get to its intended recipient - it gets caught in the Spam filters...

Beyond that we start to get in to the realms of delving around in systems and log files, something I won't go in to today!

In truth there is a whole host of things that can happen, but it is actually quite rare for e-mail to just completely vanish, I did come across an issue a few years ago, with a specific anti-virus software, if it was installed on a Mail Server, and left set to defaults it would actually cause mail that was `in transit` to be deleted, it caused me some head scratching for a while. But those kinds of things are few and far between and we have some handy tools available now to help us spot those things easier...

Some of the things we can do to help e-mail along

The Wrong Address - Pay attention to bounce backs
If you are getting a 'Message Delivery Failed' Message when sending to someone, it's a very good indication your e-mail didn't get there! Usually it's either the wrong email address, or a problem with their mail server. Similar if someone says they got a bounce back when sending to you, you need to know what that says to make sure it's not a bigger problem (i.e. it's not that they just typed the wrong address in!)

It did get there
Some people use Delivery and Read Receipts, thinking this is a good way to guarantee delivery or not, there are good and bad points for these, personally I don't like them, they create extra e-mail traffic, are more work for the email servers and can annoy some people...

Delivery Receipts – These are a bit like the postman saying "Well I put it through the letter box"

Read Receipts – these are like a reply paid envelope, it relies on someone actually agreeing to send it back.

Personally I don't use delivery or read receipts, if I want to know if someone's got my e-mail, I'll ask them to reply and let me know they've got it! (I might have given you a hint at my secret, sure fire guarantee here...)

4 quick tips for avoiding spam filters
> **Don't use Excessive Caps** – I've seen some people when they've got something urgent to ask, or because they've not had a response to their last email use ALL CAPITAL LETTERS in the subject line (and worse, sometimes the whole email too!) – this is a **fantastic** way to end up in the junk folder, don't do it!

- ➢ **Don't use broken English** (or whatever language you are using!) – Spam filters are fairly intelligent these days, they use various techniques for scanning the text content of the email, and if the text doesn't flow properly, or it doesn't make sense, it's more likely to be classed as spam.
- ➢ **Don't use excessive 'Spam words'** – I think it's pretty obvious using words like 'Viagra' will increase your chance of being identified as spam, but also words and phrases like 'Free' or 'Hot Offer' also make a difference, use them sparingly! Try [Googling Spam Keywords 2013](#)
- ➢ **Don't send loads of emails out all at the same time** – If mail servers start to see lots of emails all coming from you within a short space of time, they are more likely to block or filter you. If you need to send lots of emails out at once, you should be using professional E-Mail marketing tools.

There was one 'technical' thing I toyed about with including in this email called 'SPF'. It's really quite important at the moment, it's basically a little note for your email to say E-mail from my company is delivered from 'these places' - If it's set incorrectly, and increasingly now if it's not set, it could cause email to be dropped or at least marked as Spam.

On balance, I decided it best not to include it, and just say if you are finding a lot of your emails are not getting to where they are supposed to (especially if you are sending to Yahoo, Hotmail or the like) then it may well be an SPF issue. Give us a call and we'll take a look for you! - 01543 241 016

If you're just curious and want to know more SPF, drop me an email and I'll happily furnish you with a whole host of exciting technical facts. (at least I find them exciting!)

Shhh, this is my Secret, surefire, guaranteed way to know that you're email reached where it was supposed too…

I was a little bit worried today I might get carried away talking about email and bore you, so here's my secret tip... and do please let me know what you thought of this email!

The Number One, **Guaranteed way** to ensure your email has got to where it was supposed to get too... call the person!

Seriously, if your email is that important that you need to know they've got it, read it, and if appropriate acted on it, there is no substitute for picking up the phone...

Top Tip:

If it's a mega important e-mail, follow it up with a phone call (and ask for confirmation it's been received!)

Follow the 4 quick tips for avoiding spam filters

Giveaway #2 – Free SPF Check

If you'd like us to check if you've got SPF setup on your domain or not jump over here and we'll test it for you for free...

http://chrisbluntbooks.co.uk/freeSPFCheck

```
From: Chris Blunt chrisblunt@busstopgroup.co.uk
Sent: 11th April
```
Subject: **Can you change your password please?**

If I asked you today to go and change every password on every website you ever use, what would you say?

Ok, so what if you were told someone had just found out your password for Facebook, and they were going to go and try it on several other sites including amazon, eBay, various banks and numerous other websites. What would you think then?

Scary thought?

One more thing.

This happened. Not with Facebook, but with Sony, do you remember the news a couple of years back, Sony was all over it because their Password database got hacked, and millions of usernames and passwords were stolen from them, they were posted on the internet for all in sundry to see and abuse. In the last year alone high profile sites like Yahoo, LinkedIn, eHarmony and Last.fm have all have security breaches in their password databases.

That's why you put yourself at risk when you use the same password across every single website you use.

Before rush out and change every password you have, finish reading this email, it'll only take another minute or two, and it might give you a few pointers...

Personally, I classify the different websites I use in to 3 categories:

1. Insecure – nothing of real worth, minimal impact if someone got in;
2. Important – Would cause severe embarrassment or a lot of work if compromised;
3. Critical – Significant Financial or Business impact.

For my critical systems (like bank accounts & email accounts), I always have a different, secure password for each individual system, I would rather forget the password and ask for it to be reset than use something less secure.

For my important systems, typically things like online shopping sites, or social Media, I'll use variation passwords (groups of passwords that are similar, but not identical), and I have several of them.

For my insecure stuff, these are systems that don't have any impact on me if they were compromised, for example gaming sites (chance would be a find thing these days!), or supplier product information sites. The key thing here is there is no or very, very little risk to me if someone did access these sites. Here I have a bank of 'insecure' passwords that I pick from, then when I come to log in again, if I can't remember the right one, I just have to cycle through my list till I find the one I used...

NB: Insecure Passwords are not things like 'password1', it's a password I use in more than one place...

I also have a 4th category, and that's for times I really don't want to provide a password, or setup and account, but I'm forced to – for example when you want to comment on a website, or download a White Paper, it's rare I'll need that ever again, and if I do, I can either reset or setup a new account.

How do I remember them all?
Truth is I don't, I quite regularly have to request a password reset to some website or other, but that only takes a couple of minutes.

A thought to leave you with...
Do you use the same key for your front door, back door, windows, car, office, garage? Do you send the hotel you stay at on holiday the same key and ask them to make it open your hotel room?

Are you doing the same thing with your password?

Top Tip:

ALWAYS, use a unique password for your Banking!

ALWAYS, use a (different) unique password for your E-Mail

These two are likely your most secure systems. For anything else just think what someone could do if they knew your password for that system?

Remember, most websites have an easy password reset system that will email you through a new password or activation link in a couple of minutes. Don't get stressed about having to remember 100's of passwords, I don't!

Flick to the end of the book to find out how to get my Free guide to creating secure, memorable passwords...

From: Chris Blunt chrisblunt@busstopgroup.co.uk

Sent: 18th April

Subject: **I've noticed there is a problem with your computer.**

This is something I came first came across last summer, and it's a variation on the 'Microsoft Tech Support Scam'. I've heard of a couple more incidents lately, so it may be on the resurgence again and this time they are targeting Mac's too!

Most people will have either experienced the 'Microsoft Tech Support Scam', or know someone who has, in fact last year I had a call from my Dad. He said he'd just had Microsoft on the phone and they'd told him there was a problem with his computer, he asked them to call back in 30 minutes after he'd spoken with me.

When I spoke to him, I was surprised to learn he was fairly convinced this was real, one of the main points was they knew he had a windows computer… "Yea but Dad, *Most* people have a computer in their house with Microsoft Windows on it…"

He was called back no less than 7 times after that, in the end I told him to say he'd had his computer confiscated by me (and yes I was quite tempted too!)

Evolving the 'Microsoft Tech Support Scam'

So back to the variation that seems to be going round, the interesting point that made me take note, was they were no longer claiming to be from Microsoft, they said they were a local IT support company, the conversation went something like this…

"Hello Sir, we've noticed there is a problem with your computer, we are a local I.T. company and have been doing a scan of the local area and your computer has been identified as having a problem, would you like us to take a look at it for you?"

"erm, I'm a bit busy at the moment, can I call you back?"

"Certainly our number is 01543…."

<the usual constant callbacks then started, now they thought they might have a potential victim, and not someone who would just tell them to get stuffed.>

So to make this more believable, They had a local number to back up their story (the number they gave was the same as what Caller ID said), and they were happy to let you call them back.

The other clever part was they didn't relate it specifically to Windows, so even if you had an Apple Mac the scam would still work. As soon as you'd been to the website they asked you to, they'd then know all about your computer and could tailor the scam accordingly.

Why do they do it? Is it really worth it?

I often get asked, why do they do it? Well scams like this usually have one of 4 aims:
- Get you to install some malicious software on your machine;
- Get you to give them Remote access to your machine;
- Get you to provide your credit card details to them;
- Direct you to a website where it asks you to put in payment details.

I then also usually get asked "it seems like a lot of work, is it worth it for them?" Well these scams are usually run by large organised crime syndicates, and there is enough of it going on to make you think they are getting something worthwhile out of it?

Top Tip:

If anyone you don't know calls you up out of the blue and tells you there's a problem with your computer (or mobile phone, or iPad for that matter), just don't even entertain them. Speak to your local IT company that you know and trust.

From: Chris Blunt chrisblunt@busstopgroup.co.uk

Sent: 25th April

Subject: **Who else is using your password?**

Following on from a few recent emails on password security, I've got hold of the Top 25 passwords from 2012, I'd suggest if your password is on the list, or is even remotely similar to one on the list, then you should go and change it now!

I sent out an email a few weeks ago with tips on creating a secure, memorable password, if you want a copy then let me know and I'll forward it over to you.

Top 25 Passwords of 2012

1. password
2. 123456
3. 12345678
4. abc123
5. qwerty
6. monkey
7. letmein
8. dragon
9. 111111
10. baseball
11. iloveyou
12. trustno1
13. 1234567
14. sunshine
15. master
16. 123123
17. welcome
18. shadow
19. ashley
20. football

21. jesus
22. michael
23. ninja
24. mustang
25. password1
26. YOURNAME123

That's it for this week, Just a short one!

From: Chris Blunt chrisblunt@busstopgroup.co.uk

Sent: 2nd May

Subject: **The most useful program on my computer.**

It occurred to me after speaking to a number of people lately, that you might find it useful if I shared with you some of the useful tools and programs I use day to day, little things that make *my* life easier when working on my own computer...

What better place to start with **THE most useful program**, I use it pretty much every day, without fail (in fact I've even used it to help me write this email to you!), it is one of the most basic programs, but it's versatility just makes it so useful...

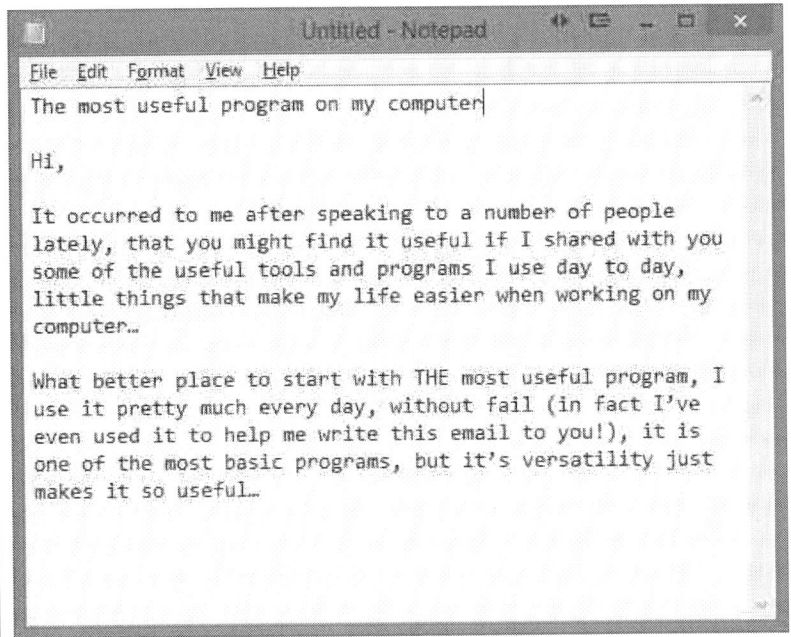

Why?
It has this amazing ability, a secret weapon if you like, I'm sure

39

there is a technical term for it, but it's probably best described as **the 'crap' filter**. You see you can dump pretty much anything in to notepad and it will strip out all formatting, fonts, colours and weird and wonderful punctuation (technically known as 'META data') leaving you with a nice clean block of text.

Some of the things I use it for on a regular basis:
- When I want to copy text from a website in to Microsoft Word – it means I can paste it in and not have to mess about with the formatting!
- When I'm coping several things at once, and I need someone to temporarily store them…
- When I only need to print a small part of an email, or document, or website, I can just paste it in to word and print it straight out, without wasting paper or toner!
- When I've written a load of content in word I want to add to my website, but I don't want all the formatting it's done.
- To keep a list of things to remember for my next meeting…

Great, so where do I find Notepad?

Now if you've not used notepad much before, you might find it's buried somewhere in your start menu. The truth is, I don't even know where it is on my start menu, and that's because there is a great short-cut to start it up…

Giveaway #3 – Free Video Tips

I'm developing a range of Video Tips, to show you step by step how to do time saving stuff with your computer… if you'd like to know more just visit:

http://chrisbluntbooks.co.uk/freeVideoTips

40

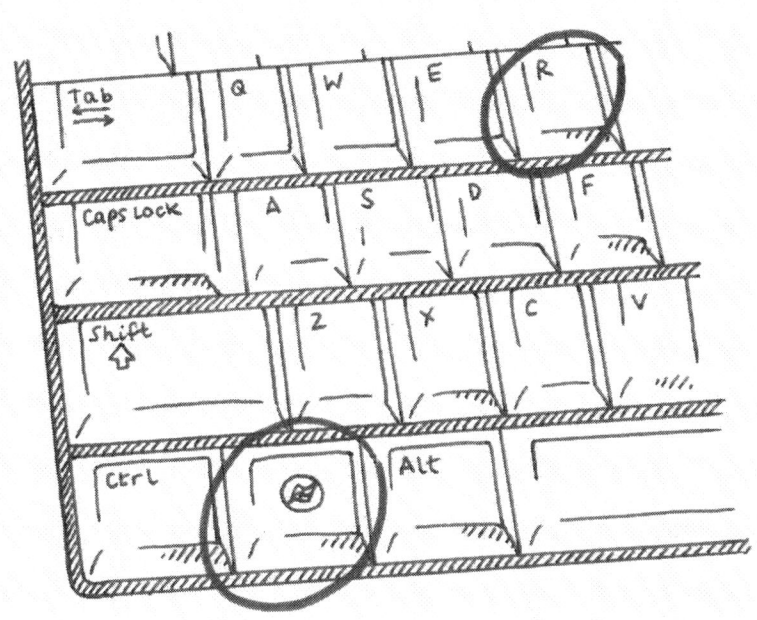

Step One: Press and Hold the 'Windows Key' Then, whilst still holding the windows key press 'R'

Up pop's the run dialogue box,

Step Two: and in there you can type 'notepad' and whack enter...

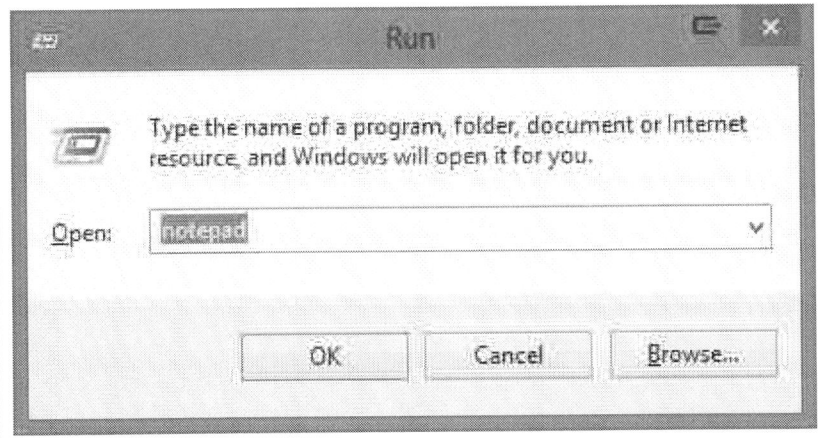

Step Three: up pops notepad...

Give it a try, then hit reply and let me know what you use notepad for...

Top Tip

If you're struggling to copy some text from a website or another document, and the formatting is going 'all weird' Fire up notepad, paste it in to there, and then copy it back out to your document...

From: Chris Blunt chrisblunt@busstopgroup.co.uk

Sent: 9th May

Subject: **Have you got a 'lifebuoy' for your business?**

It's a pretty serious topic this week, but something I've been reminded of the importance of recently.

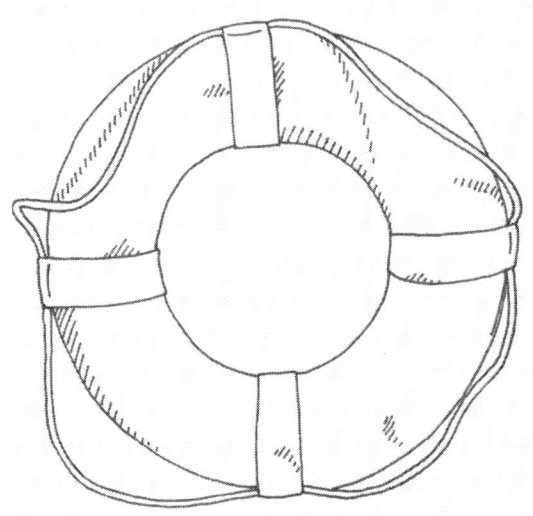

The analogy of a life ring does work quite well, you see you hope you'll never have to use one, they are supposed to be regularly checked and maintained and if kept in good working order, they do really save lives!

So what am I talking about?

Backups. **Backups are the lifebuoy of your business.**

I've seen two specific incidents lately where backups have literally saved a business.

In one incident the businesses server failed over a weekend. I don't just mean it was down for a day or two, it died completely. The data on the actual server could not be recovered, gone. The only option was to revert to backups... for everything... E-Mails, Accounts, Customer Documents, the lot... Luckily they had remote backups setup and working, and could start restoring their data straight away.

It is a scary thought, losing all your data and these incidents are very rare, but they do happen, and that's why you need backups.

So what do your backups look like? Have you got any? When did you last check them? Did you check them yourself, or are you relying on someone else?

Top Tip:

If you've not got backups - go get them now!
If you've got backups, go test them, now!
If you've got backups, and someone else looks after them for you, go check they've been tested!

From: Chris Blunt chrisblunt@busstopgroup.co.uk

Sent: 16th May

Subject: **Did you get the job?**

This one came up during a recent I.T. Clinic, we'd been talking about e-mail and computer scams, and right on cue someone received this e-mail...

Now you'll notice there are no links to click which could take you to a malicious site, and no attachments that could contain a virus... so what's the point in sending out a seemingly harmless email...

We'll it got me wondering at first, but then after reading it a bit more closely I realised it was an 'old school' scam...

Take a closer look at the phone number...
On first read it looks like a mobile number, but it's not... 070

numbers can be premium rate...

After a bit of research it seems this particular number is quite new (the first reports had been 3 days ago), one victim was actually waiting for a job interview and called it... £4.50 was his bill for that call... another was concerned the 'real' person would miss their interview chance so called up too...

Also if you happened to read this email on a mobile phone, most of them have this 'handy' feature which identifies phone numbers and makes it easy for you to click on them...

Top Tip:

Know the number you are calling... if you are unsure about the number just pop it in to Google, especially if you don't recognise the first 3 or 4 digits... Google 070

From: Chris Blunt chrisblunt@busstopgroup.co.uk

Sent: 23rd May

Subject: **It's all I seem to be talking about at the moment.**

I had a conversation with a lady 3 or 4 weeks ago who was really struggling with her e-mail... she had 4 different e-mail accounts, 2 computers in two different locations, a laptop, an iPhone and an iPad, after chatting with her for 4 or 5 minutes, she was in a real mess with her e-mail.

Since then it seems to be pretty much every conversation I've had with people has been about how they manage their e-mail across the multitude of electronic devices we find ourselves in possession of these days,

It's a bit like when you buy a new car, and then you suddenly start to notice them EVERYWHERE?

I'm not going to launch in to a whole sales pitch on Managed E-Mail Services, I know a lot of your reading this are already using them, and it's not what Top I.T. Tips is about! But if your e-mail wont let you do some of the basics below, you really should talk to someone about getting it sorted...

Some of the fundamental basics you should be able to do with your e-mail
- You should be able to see emails you've sent from your phone, on your computer;
- If you delete an e-mail on your desktop, it should also vanish from every other device you read your email on;
- If you've got staff, you should be able to see their inbox and sent items if you need to - without using their computer (NOTE: that's from an I.T. perspective, not a HR one!);

- Your e-mails should be backed up! (This is a major one, we've talked backups before...);
- If you work with a team, you should all be able to share a 'team' mailbox and know which e-mails have been dealt with;
- If you're good at filing your e-mail in to different archive folders, you should be able to view those folders when out and about on your phone and laptop;

and finally...

- you should not have to *think* about it, it should *just work*.

If you can't do or your not sure how to do any of the things below, then just ask.

The I.T. Clinic on June 6th will also have some tips on managing your email (along with the rest of Microsoft Office) - You can Book Here

Top Tip

If you've not already got a 'Hosted Exchange' E-mail account, go get one (Get a Free trial here), if you've already got one, make sure you are using it right. You should be able to send an email from your phone, and the click 'Sent Items' on your computer and see that very same e-mail.

Giveaway #4 – Free trial of Office 365

Grab a 30 days free trial for up to 10 users from

http://chrisbluntbooks.co.uk/free365trial

```
From: Chris Blunt chrisblunt@busstopgroup.co.uk
Sent: 30th May
Subject: It made me blush...
```

My apologies but it's a bit of a sobering topic this week, anti-virus... but I do promise you a couple of entertaining stories at the end to make it worth your while reading...

Whether you know it or not, there is an extremely high probability that you have had a computer virus at some point or other... or to be more correct, 'computer malware'.

I know I'm stating the obvious, but you really, really should have anti-virus protection, and it needs to be kept up to date, if you have someone monitoring it for you even better!

Yes we do still come across people who don't have anti-virus *"because it slows my computer down"* or *"it stops me opening some files"*, in which case you need to question what files you are opening, and if you are using the right anti-virus. The good ones stop most of the viruses and you barely notice they are there (**there are also some bad ones** that don't slow your machine down, but equally don't actually catch many viruses!).

So what do they do? What's the point of Viruses?
Some are purely malicious, out to cause damage and destruction to your computer and computer network. A lot of people will create these for personal recognition, to even try to get a job.

Others are designed more for monetary gain, whether it's to capture your personal details or passwords, bombard you with adverts or hold you to ransom (do you remember Top Tip #1?)

49

So what can you do about them?
As I mentioned above, having good virus protection is essential, but don't just assume because you have protection you won't get a virus.

If you notice your machine doing 'something odd' or it's suddenly gone really slow, or keeps re-directing you to random websites, you might have a virus, get it checked out.

Aside from our main managed anti-virus system, we also use something called 'Malware Bytes' to check things out. You can run it yourself, or feel free to give us a call and we can do it for you.

Mac Users, if you've heard Mac users saying they don't need anti-virus protection because Macs can't get viruses, that's not strictly true, it is possible, just far more uncommon and there are simple steps that they should take to help this. That's not the point though is it? **How impressed would your client be if you'd inadvertently forwarded them a virus just cause 'you're OK'?**

For the really stubborn viruses, a rebuild is by far the best way to ensure your machine is completely clean,

Would you be embarrassed?
Bearing in mind what I've just said, I did once have a case where I'd rebuilt the laptop, completely clean, then the very next day he came back again with the same problem, and again the next... I have to say I was a little perplexed as to how a virus could be so persistent...

That was until he gave a quick glance over his shoulder and pulled a website and said ... *"could it be coming from here"*... I don't need to tell you what was on the site, suffice to say, **it made me blush!**

I know I promised you two stories at the top, but on reflection the 2nd story is not something I think I can commit to type, I will simply say some viruses are created just to embarrass, and when I was stood in front of an office of 10 women and they ask me to look at this particular laptop I was suitably embarrassed. (I went redder than a Ferrari!)

I appreciate this has been a lengthy e-mail this week, if there is enough interest I may do a separate webinar session on this and related topics? Also, as a thank-you for reading this far, if you're not happy with your existing Anti-Virus I can offer you a month's free trial of our own Managed Anti-Virus (We look after it all for you), just reply back and let me know…

Top Tip

Make sure your anti-virus is up to date (or better still someone is monitoring it for you).
If you notice anything 'odd' with you computer, get it checked out, either run malware bytes yourself, or give us a call to look at it for you.

Giveaway #5 – Free MAV Trial

If you have concerns about your existing Anti-Virus software, or maybe you're not even using any?? Get a free 1 month trial on me…

http://chrisbluntbooks.co.uk/freeMAVtrial

From: Chris Blunt chrisblunt@busstopgroup.co.uk

Sent: 6th June

Subject: **What does your E-Mail address say about you?**

I promised last week I'd keep this one short for you, so I will, if you want more information just drop me an e-mail back and I'll be glad to help...

This week I'm asking you to think about what your e-mail address says about you, it's one of the things I see daily that for one reason or another irritates me.

The truth of the matter is, if you've got an email address that ends in hotmail.co.uk or gmail.com or btconnect.com or any other ending that is not specific to your business then what are you really saying to your potential customers?

I get dozens of e-mails daily from people trying to sell me something all sending from a g-mail or BT email address, and they all go in my deleted items, because rightly or wrongly **I don't see them as 'proper businesses'**, often your e-mail address is the first, or one of the first, impressions you make, and if it's a generic email address... it's a bad one... it just doesn't look professional.

Equally if your business card says '**sales@mycompany.com**' or 'info@mycompany.com' what are you saying to people? Hint: It's not that you're going to deliver a great personal service and personally make sure they are looked after is it?

Do you get the sense I could go on and on? (I did but then realised I'd promised to keep this short!)

> **Top Tip**

Get your own domain name, make sure it looks professional.
Check what address is on your business card, and what address you 'send' emails from.

> ## I Need your Help!
>
> As you can see I am quite passionate about this, if you see anyone struggling with a generic email address please pass them my way, I can help them get set-up with their own professional e-mail address for less than £5 a month.
>
> http://chrisbluntbooks.co.uk/properEmail

From: Chris Blunt chrisblunt@busstopgroup.co.uk
Sent: 13th June
Subject: **Who is reading your E-Mails?**

If someone asked you, would you rather your e-mail account or your bank account was hacked, what would you say?

It may seem an absurd question, but think about it a bit... how much of your life revolves around your email account? If someone gained access to your e-mail account what could they do?

Imagine for one moment someone did get in to your email...

They see an email from Amazon, check the email address you are using for Amazon, then firstly try your e-mail password to login to Amazon... (you are using a different password for Amazon and eBay than your email aren't you?) ... they then hit the 'forgot my password link' which sends an email through to your email account which... you guessed it, they already have access to... now they reset your Amazon password and go shopping... new TV, 20 DVDs and a Bike, all on your credit card, which just happens to be saved on Amazon...

How many systems do you log in to that will send a password reset to your email address? What could someone do if they gained access to those systems? Does your bank send you a password reset via e-mail?

Please don't have nightmares this week! I'm only trying to educate on the need for good passwords and security, not scare you out of using computers and the internet completely!

Top Tip

Keep your e-mail account secure. Make sure the password you use on your e-mail account is your most secure & precious, and don't use it for anything else!

(Remember Top Tip #5 - *creating secure memorable passwords*... and my free guide - http://chrisbluntbooks.co.uk/freepasswordguide/)

From: Chris Blunt chrisblunt@busstopgroup.co.uk

Sent: 20th June

Subject: **Really Sorry, but I've managed to double book**

How do **you** make sure you don't double book an appointment?

Don't you hate it when you go and book something in your diary, then get back to the office and find out someone else has just booked you in for something at the same time? Or how about when you try to book and appointment with someone and they say "Sorry my diaries at the office. Can I call you later?"

I've had quite a few conversations with people along these lines lately and there is a really easy solution.

You see I used to struggle with my Diary, I used to double book appointments. I was forever rushing to get out the office because I'd lost my diary under a mountain of paper and couldn't remember where I was going or who I was meeting... and yes, sometimes I'd write things in there in a hurry, and not be able to read it again in a weeks' time...

Then something happened, something that really made me realise I had to do something...

I let someone down, badly, not once but twice. The first time I 'forgot' the meeting (because I'd misplaced my diary) and the 2nd time I double booked them with an appointment that couldn't be cancelled... I lost their business because of it (and very good business it was!), but it was letting someone down that really hurt me.

Today my Diary is synchronised across all my devices. I can easily add an appointment when I'm out of the office on my phone, this is instantly synchronised back to the office, so if 2 minutes later Rachael takes a call and wants to book something in for me, she can, safe in the knowledge it won't be double booked. The best bit is I don't even have to think about it... If I add an appointment on my laptop, my phone will automatically remind me about it when it's due.

A simple, synchronised diary is REALLY easy to achieve, if you are already using 'Office 365' or 'Microsoft Exchange' you can already do this, just ask us and we'll show you how (Or pop along to the next IT Clinic - http://itclinic.eventbrite.com/).

Top Tip

Having a centralised diary, that is synchronised across your computer, phone and tablet really makes life easy. If you are using Microsoft Outlook try clicking 'New Meeting' and see what happens... or even click 'Meeting' on this email set the date and time to July 4th, 10am and see what happens... send it to me, I won't bite!

Giveaway #7 –I.T. Clinic Ticket

I've mentioned the I.T. Clinic a few times now, if you are intrigued and would like to come along, visit the link below and get I'll even pay for your ticket...

http://chrisbluntbooks.co.uk/itclinic

From: Chris Blunt chrisblunt@busstopgroup.co.uk
Sent: 27th June
Subject: **Missing E-Mail**

What would happen to all your email if your computer got stolen?

How do you make sure your e-mail is all backed up and what can you use to do it?

If you are already using Microsoft Exchange or Office 365 you can put a big tick in this box, your email is already all backed up for you – though you do need to **read the note on Archiving below…**

If you are using something called 'POP' or 'IMAP' it's not, and you really should think about how you back your emails up.

If you are not sure what type of e-mail you are using, you can easily check by clicking 'Account Settings' in your email (Normally under the 'File' or 'Tools' Menu) and then see what 'type' it says you've got, here what mine says…

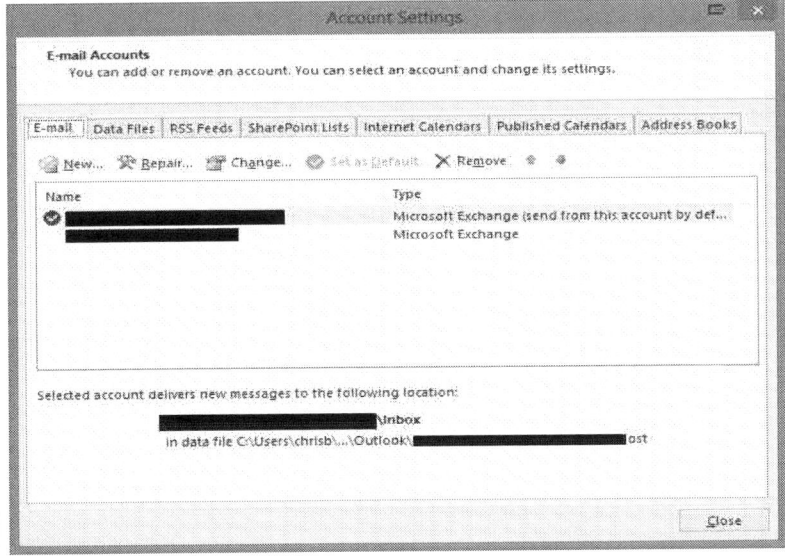

Can you see it says 'Microsoft Exchange'. That means all my email is stored on the server, I can use any computer (or phone) and I still see the same mailbox.

If it says 'POP' or 'IMAP' here, then you do need to think about e-mail backups.

The simple answer would be to move to Office 365 (which, for what we are talking about here, is the same as Microsoft Exchange). Because your email is all stored on the server, it's all backed up for you. You don't have to think or worry about anything!
The not so simple answer is to try to back up the 'PST' file yourself...

You've probably heard of a 'PST' file before, that's what both POP and IMAP use to store your email on your computer. PST files are notoriously bad for becoming corrupted, when they do, it can be a real pain to get your email back. You also need to make sure the backup software you use does 'incremental' backups of your PST file, these files can become quite large and you don't want to have to back up the whole lot every night!

A Note on Archiving...
When you hit 'Archive' in Outlook, that's removing the email from your main e-mail account and putting it in a **separate** archive file... even if you are using Microsoft Exchange or Office 365!

The trouble here is if you are using something like Microsoft Exchange, as soon as you hit 'archive' that email is not backed up any more!

My advice to you in this case would be to either not archive, just move to a separate folder within your existing mail account (You can set-up an easy rule for this, ask me how...). If you have a lot of email, use a commercial archiving service that does it automatically for you. (We run one here that archives the mail before it even gets to me, so even if I delete something by mistake, I can log in to the archive and retrieve it).

A last caveat about Exchange

It is worth mentioning as a side note that I know I've said you don't have to worry as Exchange backs it all up for you... this is assuming the people looking after your exchange server know what they are doing!

Top Tip

Honestly, if you are concerned about e-mail backups, by far and away the best thing you can do is move to Office 365. If you are not quite sure or need some help, give me a call.

Also if you need to archive you mail, look carefully at where it's archiving it too... do you need to back that archive up?

Ask a Question

As you'll have noticed, a lot of my e-mails are in direct response to questions my readers have sent in... If you've got a question of your own hope over to our facebook page and post the question!

http://facebook.com/brokenStonesIT

or if you'd rather not share it publicly send it direct to me here:

http://chrisbluntbooks.co.uk/askaquestion

From: Chris Blunt chrisblunt@busstopgroup.co.uk

Sent: 4th July

Subject: **The 2nd most useful program on my computer**

There are some programs I use on my computer almost every day, Back in Top Tip #11 I told you about the most useful program on my computer, the one I use every single day (If you missed it, click here and I'll send it to you again).

Well this one comes a close second, in fact I've used it three times just to write this email to you.

Now if you've not used this in quite a while, you are going to think I'm crazy when you find out what it is, I too was quite surprised when I re-discovered it a few years ago. It's amazing how a makeover and a few simple tweaks have transformed this tool.

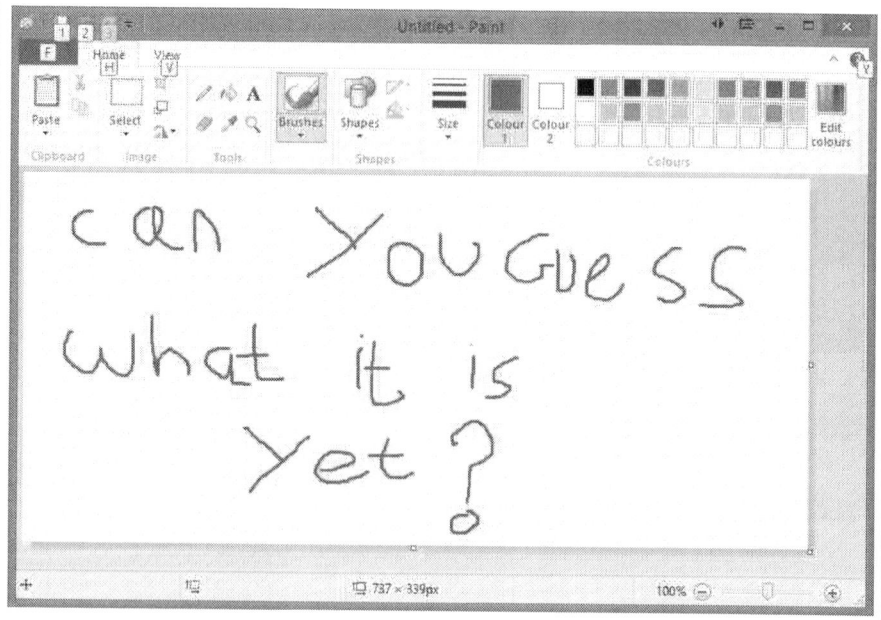

Yes, it's Good old MS Paint!!

Why do I use it so much?
For grabbing screen shots or making quick amendments to stuff, for instance if I'm writing a proposal for someone and I need to include a reference to some web content, what better way than to take a quick screen shot of it?

Or how about if you want to send on some e-mail testimonial's you've had, sure you could just copy the text, but it has a bit more impact if you take a screen shot of the actual e-mail (You can then use the shapes tool to block out the email address of mobile number of the original sender).

How to Crop
So one of the things I need to do most is 'crop' a screenshot, that's chopping out everything I don't want in the image, here's how...

Make sure the 'Select' Button it highlighted (Next to Crop), then drag your cursor around the area you want to KEEP. You'll notice a blue dotted line appear, that shows you the area you've selected... Now Hit the Crop Button (Circled in the image above), and you'll notice all but your selected area magically disappear!

Top Tip

Here's a step by step guide to taking a screenshot and e-mailing it to someone, try it now...

Press ALT + Print Screen (Takes a screenshot of your current window)

Press WINDOWS + R (Pop up the run command box)

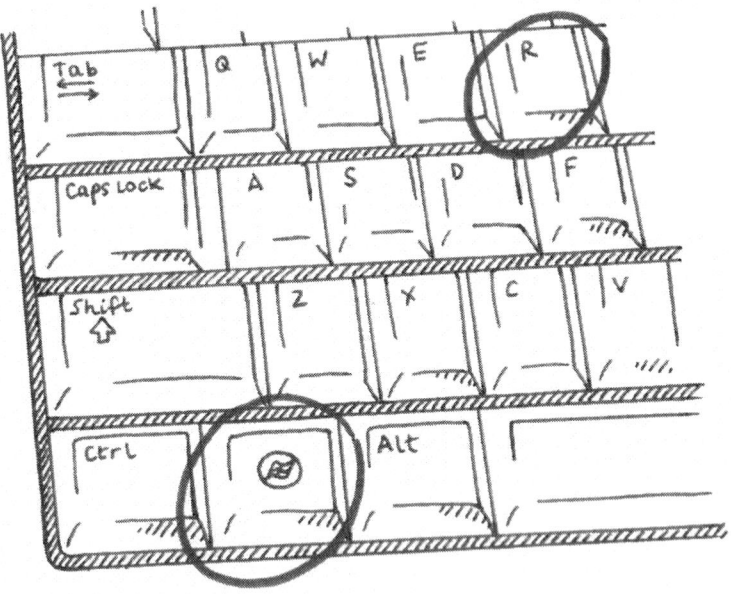

Type 'mspaint' and press enter

Press CTRL + V (Pastes the screenshot you've just taken)

Now Crop it as you want and hit Save.

If you want to capture the whole screen, rather than just the current window just press PRINT SCREEN, and if you are lucky enough to have two monitors press WINDOWS + PRINT SCREEN to capture your entire desktop!

```
From: Chris Blunt chrisblunt@busstopgroup.co.uk
Sent: 11th July
Subject:
```
 Just what does that mean?

You know when you get get those 'weird' e-mails that say they are from 'postmaster' or 'Mailer Failure Daemon', do you read them? do you understand them?

I was speaking to someone last week who had a few e-mail problems, and I asked them if they'd had any of these, their response was "Oh yea, I get loads, I just ignore and delete them"...

And then he wondered why people were not getting his e-mails...

We call these 'Bounce' Messages, an e-mail from a mail server to say it had some difficulty delivering an e-mail for you, and 'usually' what the problem was... and contrary to the belief of this particular person, they do actually mean something. They are worth paying attention to, even if you just save it to pass on to your I.T. Guy.

Every mail server is different, and may send out slightly different messages, but what's worth looking for and paying attention to is the Response Reason, these usually have a number like 5.0.0 or 5.7.1 before them and then may say something like...

```
Mailbox disk quota exceeded
```
 - (The users mailbox is full!)

or

```
No records found for: janglepr.com
```
 - (The domain name is probably wrong)

These messages are gold dust for us IT guys, and if you've got these handy when you call up for IT support we will love you for it...

Top Tip

Pay Attention to any 'unable to deliver e-mail' messages that you get, they usually mean that important e-mail you just sent, didn't get there and they 'usually' do actually tell you why.

If it's a REALLY important e-mail call the person to check to see if they got it or not... and of course if you're not sure what's what, give me a call! (HINT: Having the unable to deliver message handy would be VERY useful...)

```
From: Chris Blunt chrisblunt@busstopgroup.co.uk
Sent: 18th July
Subject: I thought we had a meeting?
```

How many times have you supposedly booked a meeting and then one of you hasn't turned up, or thought it was a different day or time?

There is a really great and easy way to avoid this, use 'Meeting Invitations' in outlook (it's not just outlook either, most decent Mail Clients have this feature too, it just might be called something else).

They are dead simple to use, and really quite effective. It even makes it easy to re-schedule the meeting if you need too…

Here's how they work…

Let's assume someone's just sent you an email to say "Are you free next Wednesday or Friday to meet?"

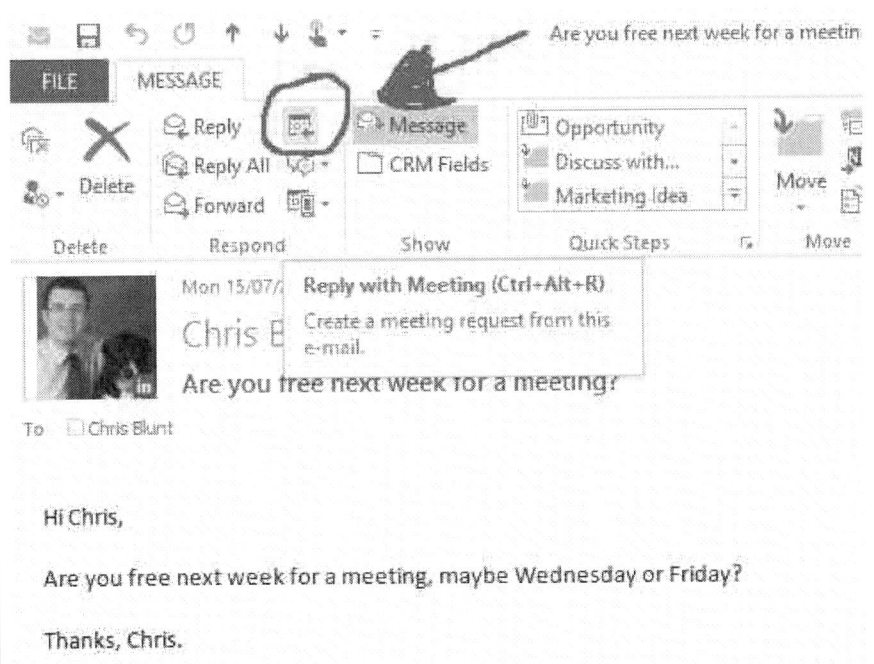

There's a little button that says 'Reply with a Meeting', click this and then up pops the Meeting request window, already filled in with their email address and subject, you just need to pick a time and date...

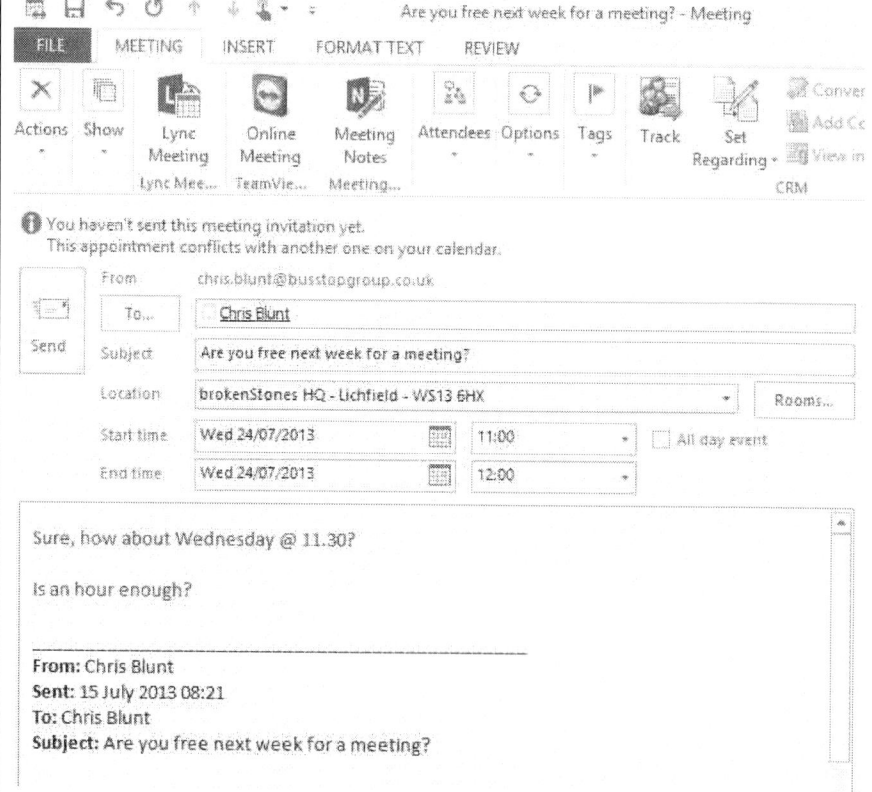

As soon as you hit send, the meeting goes in to your calendar (and if you've got Office 365 it's going to be synced with your phone, tablet and anything else that connects to your email account!).

The other person gets a meeting request, they can choose to either 'Accept', 'Propose a new time' or 'Decline', and you'll see their response in your calendar too... This is really handy when you've invited several people, knowing who's confirmed and who's not...

Another great feature is if you need to change the time, you simply edit the meeting in your calendar and the other person will get an update...

If it's you that wants to schedule the meeting, and you don't have an email to reply to, then just pick the date / time in your calendar and then look for the 'Invite Attendees' button, that gives you an extra field to put the e-mail address of the people you'd like to invite to a meeting in...

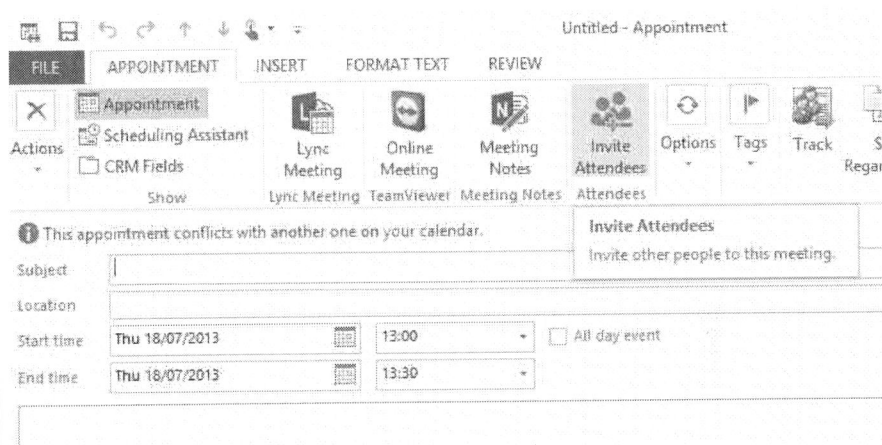

So go and give it a go now... try booking your next few meetings in this way. I find it much easier to keep track of, amend and know my meetings are properly scheduled... and if you get someone saying their e-mail won't support meeting requests, refer them my way and I'll help them out!

Oh and before you ask, yes I do often schedule meetings with myself! It's a great way to make sure some of that important 'running a business' stuff gets done without interruptions...

Top Tip

Try using the Outlook 'Meeting Requests' to schedule your meetings and help avoid missed or cancelled meetings. If someone books a meeting with you, and doesn't send a meeting request, send them one back to confirm and make sure they don't stand you up!

From: Chris Blunt chrisblunt@busstopgroup.co.uk

Sent: 25th July

Subject: **What do you mean it's not backed up?**

Imagine if your entire phone got wiped today... have you got everything on there backed up? How quickly could you get back up and running again?

Now, if you've got an iPhone, and you've got iCloud backup set-up, it's minutes... even if you lose your phone, you can restore everything back to a new phone in minutes... I'm sure it's just as easy on an Android or Windows phone..

OK, so if you've got your email set-up properly (I.E. Office 365 or MS Exchange) then getting your Mail, Contacts and Calendar back is pretty easy, but what about all your settings, and all your apps, any notes you've made... re-downloading all your music and any photos you've taken?

I've got photos of Donald going back to when he was a puppy on my phone (yes and of course both my daughters too). The rest of the stuff on my phone I can either do without or get back with some effort, but I'd be pretty upset if I lost those precious photos.

Here's how we setup Backup on your iPhone

Go in to Settings and Choose 'iCloud'

In the iCloud Menu scroll down to the bottom and choose 'Storage and Backup'

The next screen tells you how much space you are using, and how much you have available, you then just need to make sure that 'iCloud Backup' is ON.

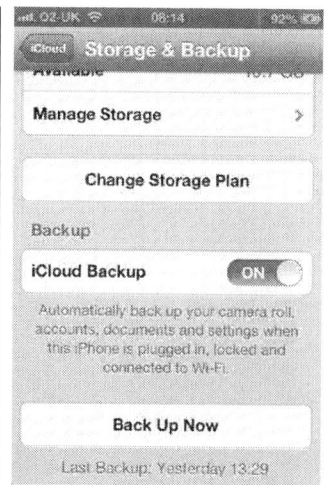

Also just below the Back Up Now button it tells you when you last backed up... it's a simple as that... now whenever your phone has WiFi and is plugged in it will automatically back itself up.

Side Note: Recently I ran out of space on my 'iCloud' I spent 2 or 3 weeks going through trying to delete stuff I didn't want / need... then I realised I was being pretty stupid! It was £28 to add an extra 20GB to my existing free 5GB, how much time had I already wasted? £28 for the year was nothing, it took less than a minute to set-up, and now I've got more space than I can use, and I've got peace of mind again...

Top Tip

Make sure you've got backup enabled on your phone right now, it's easy and it's free, and it all happens without you having to do anything! (You can also do the same thing on your iPad too!).

I've not used a Samsung phone, but I'm sure it'll be just as simple (and I'm sure someone will email with how to set it up on there too).

```
From: Chris Blunt chrisblunt@busstopgroup.co.uk
Sent: 1st August
Subject: I think there is a problem
with your website?
```

I've seen this a few times now, when the webpage loads it's either completely blank, or only half loaded, and it doesn't work properly...

The first instinct is to blame the owner of the website, they've not been looking after it properly...

But it's not always their fault... this actually happened to me last week. I e-mailed someone to helpfully point out there was a problem with their site, but there wasn't... it was all to do with me and my computer... oopps.

You see websites are getting more and more complicated, not to use or look at (that's getting better thankfully), but in the way they are constructed, and the code they use behind the scenes. Sometimes different websites can conflict with each other, or if one site has been made particularly badly, it can affect other sites (This is what happened to me, another, large worldwide company's site I was on was causing another site to run extremely slowly – like 3 seconds to load a single page...).

If you're finding trouble using a particular site there are a couple of things you can check quickly before blaming anyone else...

Either start up a different web browser (i.e. if you're using Chrome, try Internet Explorer or Firefox) or most browsers now had a handy little feature called 'In Private Browsing'.

It effectively creates a new web browser that doesn't share any of the resources from other pages you've got open... it also doesn't save any of your info or the history of what you've looked at (Handy if you are shopping for Birthday Presents!)

In **Chrome**, Click the Settings Button (the 3 lines) in the top right corner, then Click 'New Incognito Window'...

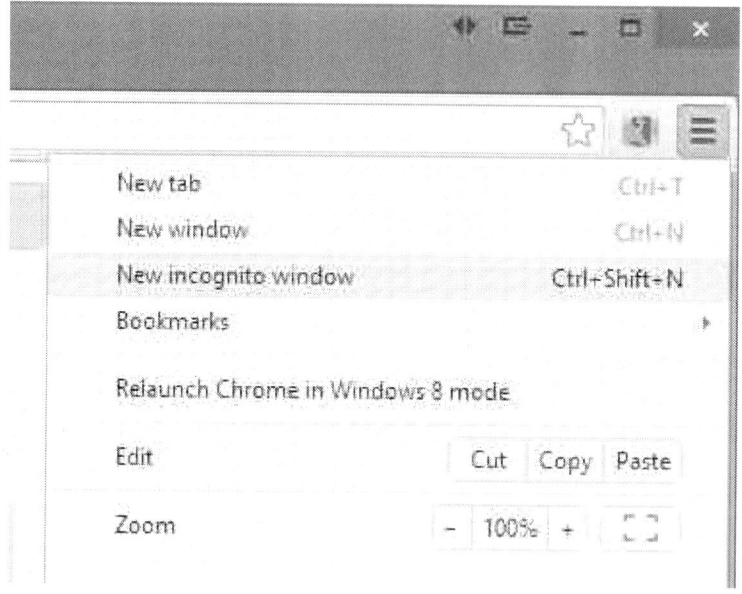

In **Internet Explorer**, Click the Cog in the top right corner, then Safety and InPrivate Browsing...

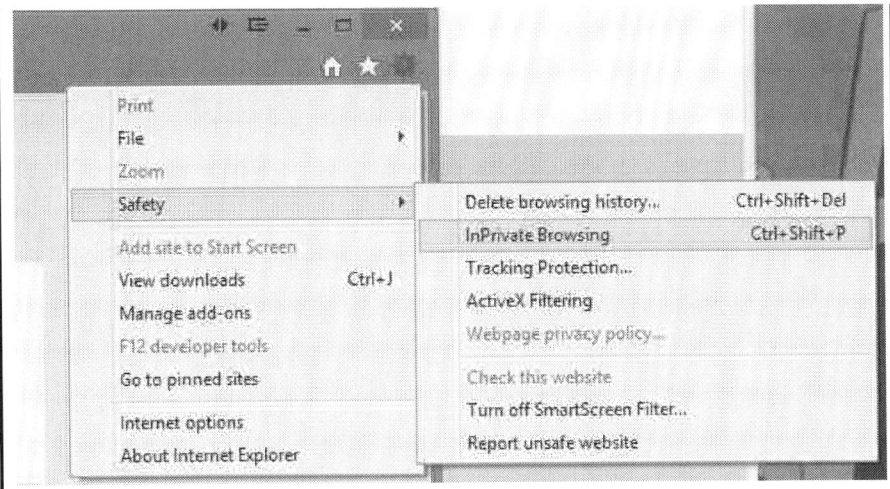

In **Firefox** Click the Orange Firefox menu the top LEFT, then Click Start Private Browsing...

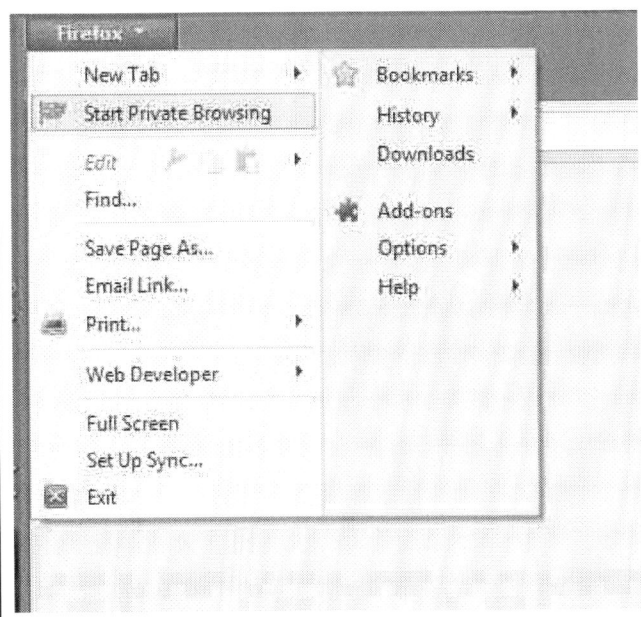

When you've done that you'll either see a new window appear (as in Chrome & IE) or the window will change (FireFox) and you should see an indication you are in Private Browsing Mode...

In Chrome you get a little 'Spy' like Man appear in the top left,

In IE you get a 'InPrivate' icon at the start of the address bar,

In FireFox the logo turns Purple...

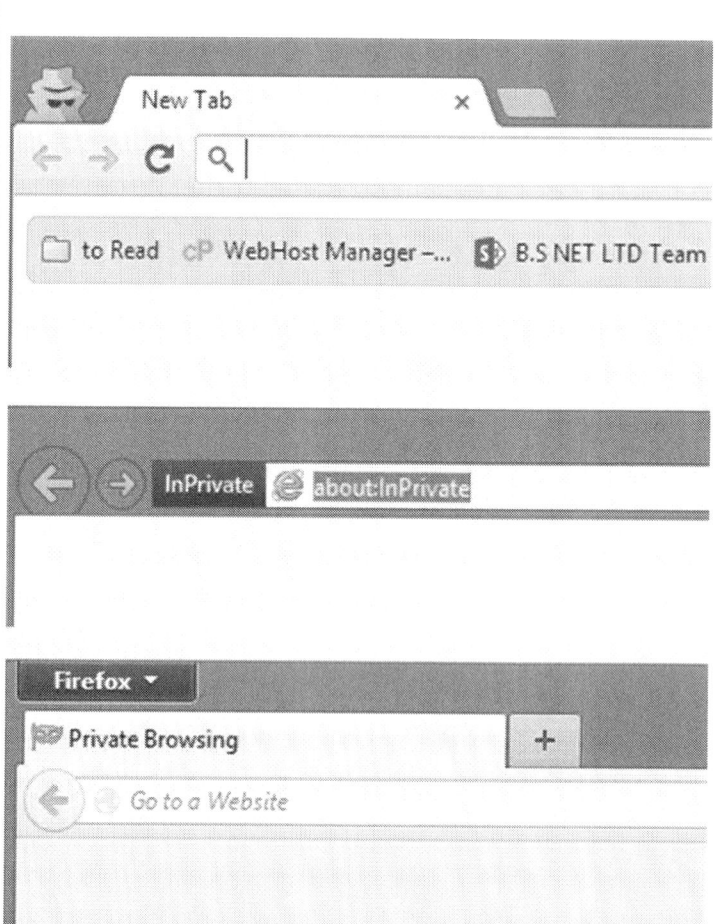

Top Tip

If you're struggling with a website not working properly... first try the InPrivate Browsing mode or another web browser to check it's not you!

Also don't forget one of the main purposes of InPrivate browsing is to keep what you're looking at secret from other users of your computer... Perhaps someone should have mentioned that to my wife before she ordered my new tennis bag for my birthday... (of course it didn't help she left it on the front seat of her car for 2 days either!)

From: Chris Blunt chrisblunt@busstopgroup.co.uk

Sent: 8th August

Subject: **Just checking you got the attachment?**

How many times have you sent or received an email that says "Please see the attached file for details..."

And there is no file attached??

I do it at least 2-3 times per month... (And that's even now that Outlook points out half the time there is no attachment... click happy!)

Using e-mail to send file attachments is great in *some* circumstances, but more often than not it can be a very **BAD** way to send files...

Why? I'll give you 3 reasons why...
- E-mail is one of **the** most inefficient ways to transmit files. You see e-mail sends everything in plain text... and I mean everything.. even that nicely compressed zip file that your computer has spent ages squeezing every last bit of space out of. E-mail takes it and bloats it up again... I'm not going to go in to the techno-babble of why this is the case, just take it from me it is.
- **Imagine you are collaborating on a file with someone**, you send them what you've done, they send you back some amendments, you tweak it and send it back again... That's just one file right? **Wrong** it's at least 8 (Assuming you both only save it once to your computer)... it's sat in your sent items twice, your inbox Once, your collaborators inbox twice, their sent items once and in both of your my documents...
- **If the file you send is more than just a few megabytes** it may well be dropped by the recipients mail server without either of you ever knowing. Some mail servers are set-up to not pass files of more than

10meg (or less!), and with Reason 1 above your file may only show 5mb, but once it's been 'bloated' it can easily double in size...

Arrgg! So how am I going to send these really important files?
There are loads of great ways to share files, it really depends on your circumstances and security requirements, but a great start is the free tool called '[DropBox](#)'

If you've not already heard of it, Drop Box creates a folder on your computer that you can save files in to... you can then choose to share that folder with selected people... you can then copy your file in to that folder and whenever you edit it. The other person gets notified and can see those changes straight away...

I use drop box for sharing files with my designer, with my mastermind group, with my VA and with my family (it's a great way to share our family photos too).

If you've not already tried Drop Box, Give it a go now and sign up [here](#) it's Free!

Giveaway #9 – 500MB Dropbox Space

If you're not already using DropBox use my referral link and get an extra 500MB for free

http://chrisbluntbooks.co.uk/dropbox

Top Tip

Save your email for sending messages, not sharing files. If you've got a large file to share with someone, try DropBox or a similar file sharing tool. It's dead easy to send them a link to a dropbox folder, plus you'll know when they've joined the folder too.

Also remember Drop box is a great way to **share** files, it's definitely NOT a way to back them up, you should have a proper remote backup solution for that (Ask me if you're unsure!)

Oh and big thanks to Karen who sent in the idea for this weeks Top Tip...

```
From: Chris Blunt chrisblunt@busstopgroup.co.uk
Sent: 15th August
Subject: Really, what's the point of
E-Mail signatures?
```

Before we start, I'll make this clear, **this is not any kind of discussion or advice on what you should legally have on your e-mails**, go speak to a Solicitor for that (I know a good one if you are struggling!).There are however many that say that if you are a limited company you must have your Registered Name, Number, Place and Address on there (as with your letterheads, website, order forms etc.)

I also make no apologies if this comes across as a bit of a Rant today, Stupid E-mail signatures are one of my bug bears... **if you are easily offended you'd probably do best to stop reading now!**

Now I'm aware I have ranted on somewhat below, so I opted not to include **my guide on how to set-up your signatures in outlook**, you can download that as a handy PDF here instead.

You will have noticed yourself there are a huge range of e-mail signatures out there, some-people don't have one at all, others take up two screens worth with logo's, disclaimers and whatever else.

Rant #1 - Why have so ridiculously long e-mail signatures that it dwarfs all but the War and Peace style e-mails? It's really annoying when you are reading through a series of e-mails which is mostly one or two liners interspersed with 30 lines of legal mumbo jumbo telling you who cant and can't read the email. Oh and BTW, for anyone who puts at the bottom "Only to be read by the intended recipient", I'm afraid I've already read it by the time I get there, so what's the point? (that's **Rant #2).**

My personal opinion, if your email signature takes up more than a quarter of a printed page it's too big, it's also not great when it's included more than once in an e-mail, (that's **Rant #3)** - **use a separate Signature for Replies**, stripped down, you can always change it if you need too... (I've created a guide for how to set-up and use your signatures in Outlook Download it here)

Rant #4 - People that don't have ANY e-mail signature. I refer back to my emails a lot for contact details, maybe I'm trying to call you myself, or maybe I need to pass your details on... so when there is no phone number or other contact details, it just makes it that bit harder to contact you...

Rant #5 - People that put their E-Mail signature FIRST... why? We are conditioned to look above the signature line for the email content, so it just looks like a blank email at first glance... anything I have to scroll down for is less likely to get my full attention (I think marketing people call it above the fold or something?) If all I see 'above the fold' is your big logo, I'm not very enticed to keep reading and scroll down...

I saved my favourite for last...

Rant #6 - Don't you find it slightly ironic when some-people put on the bottom of their e-mail **"Please consider the environment before printing this e-mail"**, that when you do print their e-mail that very line ALWAYS causes a 2nd page to be printed! Really, do many people print e-mails just for fun? Have you ever read a line like that, stopped and thought... "Hmm on balance maybe I won't print this e-mail?" I haven't, all it's ever done for me is use more paper, ink and take up more space on my screen! (I did warn I might rant a bit)...

So here's in my personal Opinion of what you should have on your e-mail signature (Please refer to paragraph one, this is NOT any kind of legal advice).

- Your Name (Yep, I've had e-mails from 'info@company' that I don't know who haven't signed their name before!)
- Your Contact Details (Phone, Web, Social Media)
- Your Company Name and a SMALL logo
- Your Registered Address & Reg number (if Limited)
- A Funky Strapline (keep it short!)

And don't forget you can get my Handy guide for setting up your E-Mail Signatures here

Giveaway #10 – Signature Guide

Download my handy free guide on how to set your e-mail signature in Microsoft outlook

http://chrisbluntbooks.co.uk/signature

Top Tip

Set-up your e-mail signatures in your Mail Client, and set a different, more compact signature for your reply - Remember you can always override it!

As my own personal E-Mail signature says **"Save Bandwidth, don't use Long winded E-Mail signatures!"**

From: Chris Blunt chrisblunt@busstopgroup.co.uk
Sent: 22nd August
Subject: **What next...**

If you've done a few presentations in your life, you'll have been in this situation before... you start talking about the next slide, only it's not the next slide, and now you've thrown yourself off track, get all confused, and if it's a bad day, your entire presentation falls apart and you feel like an idiot in front of everyone...

So did you know about **Presenter mode** in PowerPoint? When you are hooked up to a projector or a TV screen on your laptop, whilst the main presentation shows on the projector screen, you can see what's coming up next on your laptop screen... you can even see your slide notes if you wish!

#

The Left hand box shows your current slide, the right hand side shows your next slide or animation with your notes at the bottom...

You can drag between the left and right panes to resize each one, and the same with the notes...

Whats more at the top left it tells you how long you've been going...

In order to use Presenter Mode you need a couple of things setup...

Firstly you need to make sure Presenter Mode is enabled in Power point (it usually is by default, but just in case...)

Look for the 'SlideShow' Tab in the Ribbon, and then make sure the 'Use Presenter View' is ticked...

Secondly you need to make sure when you are hooked up to the Project your screen is set to 'Extend' Mode... This enables

Windows to show different things on each screen (Stating the obvious, but it 'Extends' your desktop on to two screens...)

Most laptops have hot keys for this, you usually hold down the 'Fn' key and press one of the function keys (sometimes it says 'CRT/LCD' sometimes it looks a bit like a computer screen), but windows also has a Hot Key for this... Try Pressing the Windows Key and 'P' and you'll get something like this up...

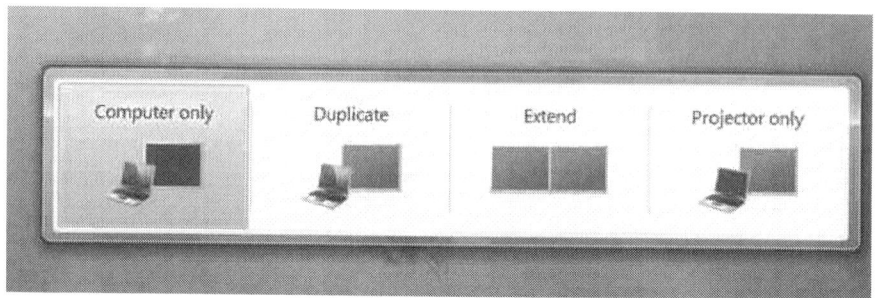

You want to choose 'Extend', just keep Holding the windows Key and tapping P till you get there, then just let go and press enter.

Top Tip

Using the Presenter Mode in PowerPoint is a great way to reassure yourself of what slide is coming up next. I also tend to use the Notes Section to add my Trigger words in so I know what to talk about if I get lost too...

```
From: Chris Blunt chrisblunt@busstopgroup.co.uk
Sent: 29th August
Subject: Unbelievable Photo
```

I quite often take photos when I'm on a clients site, sometimes it's for reference (so we know what their server room looks like, or how the cables on their router are connected up), sometimes it's of a shocking site that I'll write a blog or article about...

And an iPhone is great for this, really great, but **how do you get the photos off?** It's not like there is a memory card you can easily slot in to your computer...

Well up until recently **I used to e-mail them to myself**... I know, after everything I've said about how **e-mail is a really bad way to transfer files**... but we do what's easiest don't we? It's quick and simple, and to waste a load of time trying to transfer the photos off another way would just be plain stupid.

Then I got thinking, you know how when you take a photo on your iPhone, it **automatically gets synced** to your iPad via iCloud. **What if there was a program that did the same for your PC?** Turns out there is!
http://www.apple.com/uk/icloud/setup/pc.html

If you've got Office 365 my recommendation would be to **un-tick Mail**, Contacts, Calendar as Office 365 is already doing this for you, just l**eave Bookmarks and Photo Stream ticked**.

Once you've installed it you'll get 'Photo Stream' Appear in Windows Explorer, and from there you can s**imply drag and drop your photos** in to your articles or whatever you need them for.

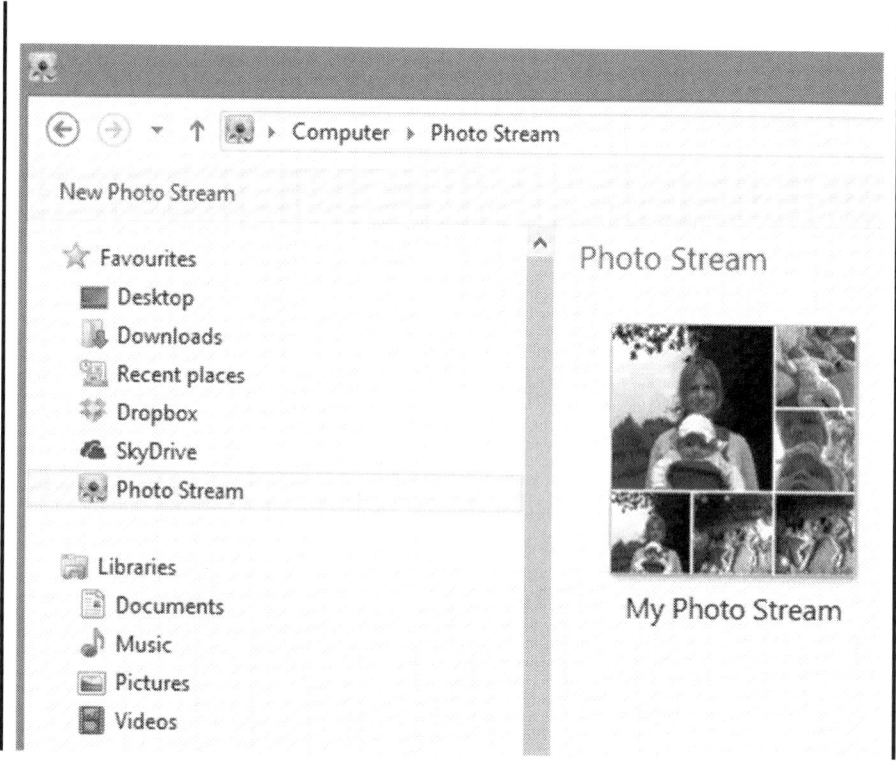

Top Tip

If you've got an iPhone, make sure you've installed iCloud on your computer (http://www.apple.com/uk/icloud/setup/pc.html) it makes syncing and accessing your photos MUCH quicker and simpler...

```
From: Chris Blunt chrisblunt@busstopgroup.co.uk
Sent: 5th September
```
Subject: **It's just a copy... a good one, but still just a copy...**

A Few Weeks ago I sent out an e-mail about how great Drop Box is for **sharing** files with others, off the back of that I've had a few people ask **how you backup your files that are stored in Drop Box? (If you Missed it, check back to page 76)**

Which on the one hand is a **great question**, cause it shows they are conscious of the **need to backup their data** (Something so many people overlook till it's too late), but on the other hand they are **missing the point of drop box** a little bit...

I'm also aware there are some people out there that think that **Drop Box *IS* a backup solution.**

It's Not.

Anything that lets you edit or change it's content when it's in it's supposed 'backed up' state, is **not a proper backup solution.**

A **proper** backup solution takes a copy of your data at a moment in time, and doesn't allow that to be changed, the only thing you should be able to do with that backup is restore it to either it's original location or an alternative one. This is to be able to preserve the integrity of the data, to be able to prove at a specific moment in time this is what my data looked like (there are many reasons why that's important, but I'd probably put myself to sleep, let along you, if I discussed them right now!) So in answer to the original question, **how do you backup your** files in drop box?

Well, **how do you backup the rest of your files?** Drop Box should be a COPY of your files, not the only or original version, if a file is important enough to be backed up, then **put it in your normal file structure** and make it **part of your normal backup** procedures...

You do have a 'normal' backup procedure don't you??

Top Tip

Drop box is a great way of Sharing files amongst your colleagues and associates when you're not all under one roof. But it's not a Backup Solution. Put a 'Copy' of the files you want to share in Drop box, not the original, make sure that's in your usual file management system and backed up in the normal way.

(Bonus Top Tip - If you've not got a decent backup system right now, make it top priority for today!)

From: Chris Blunt chrisblunt@busstopgroup.co.uk
Sent: 12th September
Subject: **The Easiest way to remember your password**

This is somewhat of a controversial topic, and I know some people are going to think I am completely mad for even suggesting it...

But **have you thought about writing some of your passwords down?**

Hardened security experts would no doubt say that this is a big No No, but today I'm going to **put a case forward for why writing it down may not be such a bad thing**...

Let's be clear, having a big sign stuck to your monitor that says **my computer password is 'rover14',** not a great idea!

You might as well not have one at all if that's what you are going to do... and you also need to realise **this is not a blanket rule for all passwords and all systems**.

You will have seen in the films where the spy breaks in to the executive's office, rifles through the files and finds the password for the computer with all the company secrets on. And yes, **that is pretty dumb**.

But many of the systems that we logon to now are accessed over the internet, and it's **rare that someone breaks in to your office to steal your password for amazon** or iTunes.

It's these types of passwords that I'm saying you would be **better off having a strong password written down, than a weak one that you remember**.

You have to think about **where the greatest threat is coming from?** Someone guessing your pets or children's names and birthdays (**have you talked about your Pets, or children on Facebook** btw? you know, wishing them happy birthday?) or someone breaking in to your office and rifling through your papers, then linking that to your online accounts?

So, if it's a **choice between** having a **really simple password like <yourname>1** vs writing down a **cryptic password like 'gV5jjd74g'** and sticking it to the underside of your drinks coaster **I'd choose the drinks coaster option**. Because the **chances are far greater of someone guessing my simple password** vs breaking in to my office and stealing my drinks coaster just to login to my amazon account.

One last note, If you do choose to write some passwords down, **make sure that you use a different password for each website you login to**, that way if one does get compromised then it's only one at risk, that you have to change and dozens...

ACTION: - I'm interested to find out what you think on this, have I made a compelling case for writing some passwords down? Let me know on the brokenStones Facebook page if you agree, or if you've got something more to add (for or against!) leave me a comment...

Top Tip

Don't use simple 'dictionary' word passwords or any names (even if it's not even family names, password cracking 101 starts with a list of words and names). The best passwords have no resemblance to words or names and look completely random.

```
From: Chris Blunt chrisblunt@busstopgroup.co.uk
Sent: 19th September
Subject:
```
Are you going to fix it, or just ignore it?

You are happily working away on your computer and then up pops a big warning box to say you've got a Virus... what do you do? Click the 'Fix Now' button, or ignore it?

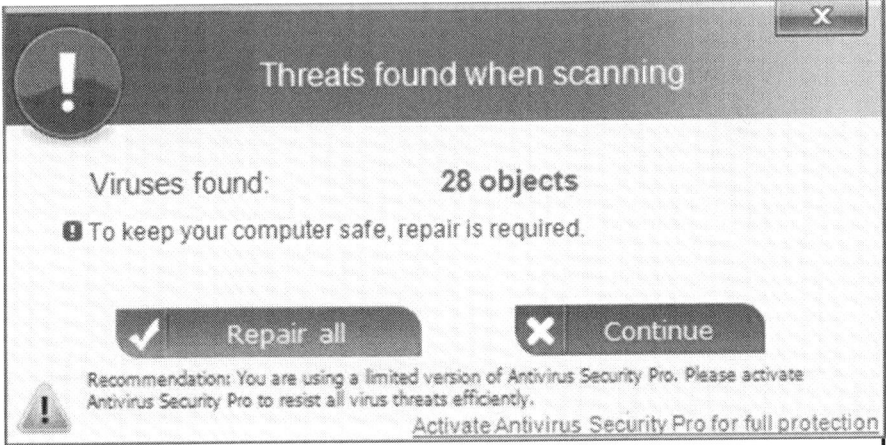

Wrong answer, you really should pick up the phone and call your IT support provider!

SCAM WARNING: This e-mail contains details of a Virus scam experienced by one of our clients recently. Fortunately they had the good sense to call us, rather than make any attempt to solve the issue on their own.

Please take heed and don't fall victim to this type of scam, as I know people have in the past.

AntiVirus Security Pro - if you see a screen like this pop up on your computer, then you've got this virus.

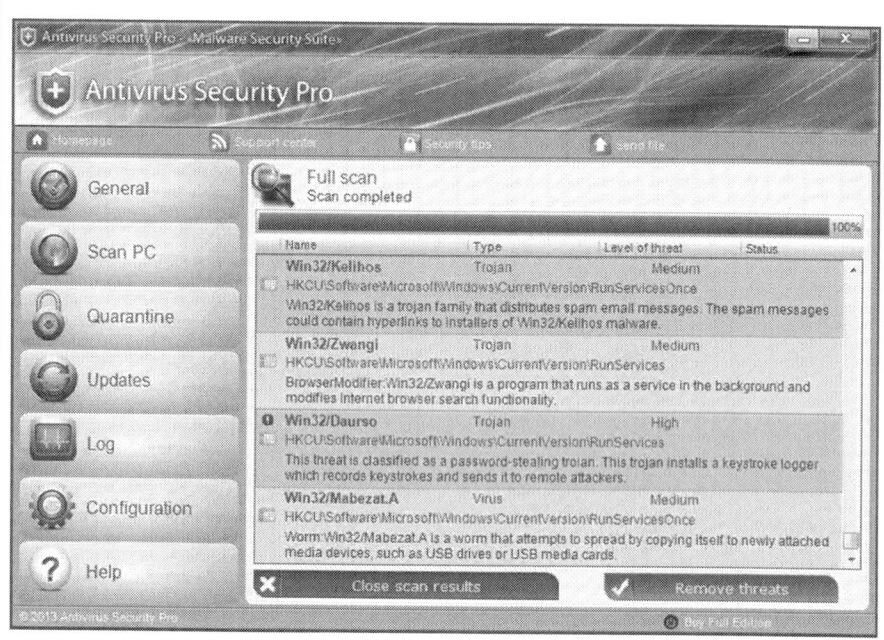

This particular virus is an extortion type virus, it's main aim is to get you to hand your credit card details over.

It presents itself as some virus protection software, telling you that you've got 100 or so viruses, and to clean them up you need to upgrade to the 'Full Edition' for about $30.

Of course it's a scam, it's all to get your card details.

(If you have already seen this or similar, and put your card details in, call your bank and stop your card now!)

It then proceeds to interfere with almost everything on your computer, every time you try to open any document or program it will pop up and pester you stopping you from doing anything, and generally causing a nuisance.

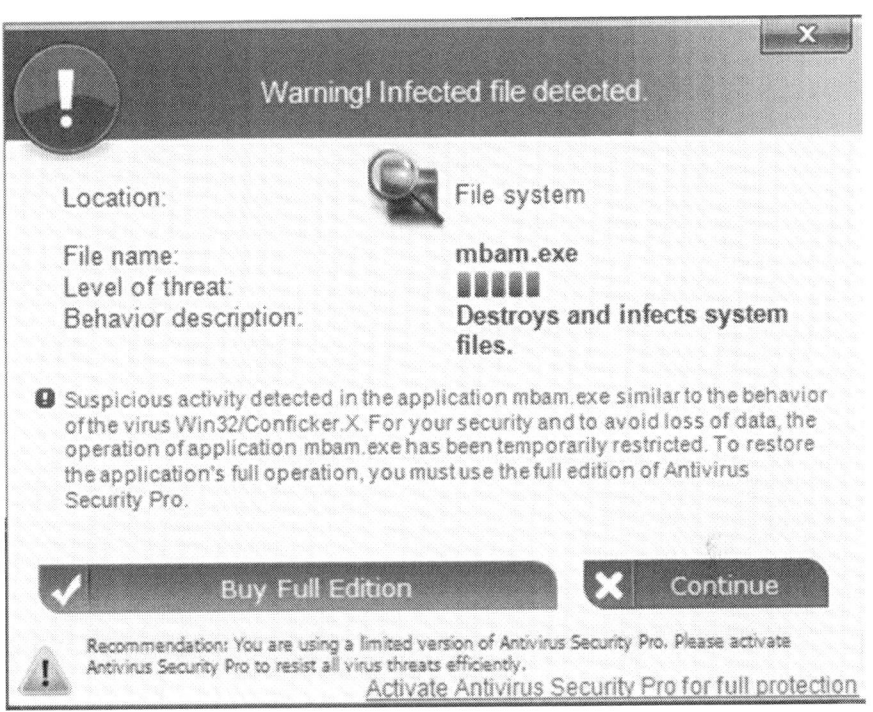

We also found that it had hidden all of 'My Documents' and then tried to trick you in to running another program to further infect your computer.

This seems to be particularly persistent virus, in the course of cleaning it up, it infected two of our memory sticks (we keep a handful of clean USB sticks, just for jobs like this!)

Please don't fall victim to this! and please pass this on to anyone else you think may find it useful.

> **Top Tip**

If you have a piece of software that pops up on your computer and you are not 100% sure about what it is, then call your Local IT Expert about it. (You can call us on 01543 241 016).

Also, a great tool to run if you are unsure about something on your computer is Malwarebytes - http://www.malwarebytes.org - if it doesn't run for any reason, you really should call an expert!

NOTE: Some of you may be wondering why this virus wasn't stopped by their existing Anti-Virus Software, well the truth is that no anti-virus software is 100% effective, some things do get through, no matter what anti-virus software you use.

From: Chris Blunt chrisblunt@busstopgroup.co.uk
Sent: 26th September
Subject: **Isn't that *your* domain name?**

I routinely come across businesses which don't own their own domains, they might think they do and the company they registered it through might tell them it is, but have you actually checked?

Why is it important I own my domain name?

It never really becomes an issue until you fall out with someone. I have known plenty of people who's domain names have been in the name of their web developer, or one of the directors of the business, it's all been fine for years, but then for one reason or another there is a falling out, someone decides to get vindictive, and they cause trouble... sure when it comes down to it, and you go to court you might be able to prove it should actually be yours, or the companies, but do you really want all that hassle and cost when it takes less than a minute to check, and only a few minutes to change it, if it's wrong?

I've also heard of it cause complications when you come to sell your business, and let's face it your website and on-line presence is only becoming more important... it's such an easy thing to do, and so often over looked...

So how do I check if I own it myself?

It's really simple to check, pop over to our own WhoIs Tool, Enter your domain in the box at the top, then type in the annoying code (sorry, but the number of people I had abusing this I had to put the capture code in!), then hit 'Submit'

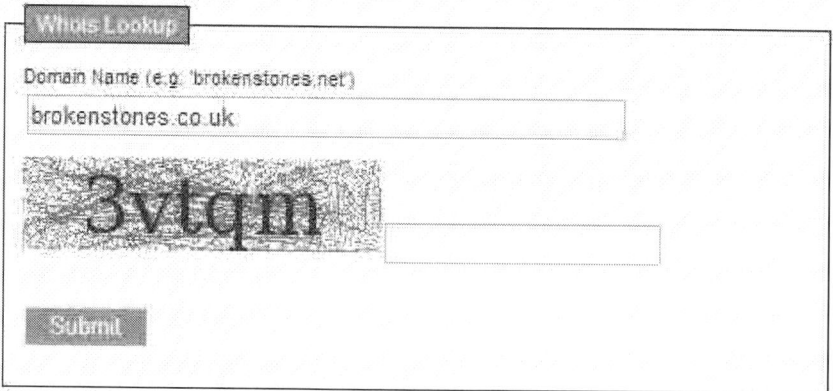

If you've typed your domain name in correctly (yes, I did type mine wrong first time! and it took me a moment to realise - ever get the feeling it's going to be one of them days?), you should then see some results showing you all the public information about your domain name, you want to look for where it says 'Registrant' - that's you!

```
brokenstones.co.uk
Domain name:
brokenstones.co.uk

Registrant:
brokenStones Limited

Registrant type:
UK Limited Company, (Company number: 5926376)

Registrant's address:
Bridge House
Station Road
Lichfield
WS13 6HX
United Kingdom

Registrar:
B S Net Ltd t/a The Busstop Group [Tag = BSNET]
URL: http://www.busstopgroup.co.uk

Relevant dates:
Registered on: 29-Jun-2009
Expiry date:   29-Jun-2015
Last updated:  01-Jul-2013
```

If it's not got your name, or your company name, it means it's not technically yours! You really should get it updated.

So why is the domain not registered correctly to start with?

From experience I know that some people simply don't realise when they register the domain they should enter it in the owners name as opposed to theirs, but then there are probably also companies out there who purposely register it in their own name to try to keep some sort of control over their client.

How do I change it to my name?

97

To change a the 'registrant' of a .uk domain currently costs £10+VAT see details on nominet for more details.

For most of common domain extensions (like .com, .net, .org) it's normally free to update your details, you just need to contact whoever looks after your domain for you.

Top Tip

Go and check that you own all your domains names now. It's quick and it's simple

If it's not got your name in the 'Registrant' Field, go and get it updated today...

Giveaway #11 – Do you own your own domain?

Use my free domain checker to find out who is actually listed as the owner of your domain name

http://chrisbluntbooks.co.uk/whois

```
From: Chris Blunt chrisblunt@busstopgroup.co.uk
Sent: 3rd October
Subject: Conned Again
```

I guess it must be the lure of free money, as It's not the first time that I've written about this, and I'm sure it won't be the last. It keeps on happening, and people keep on falling for it!

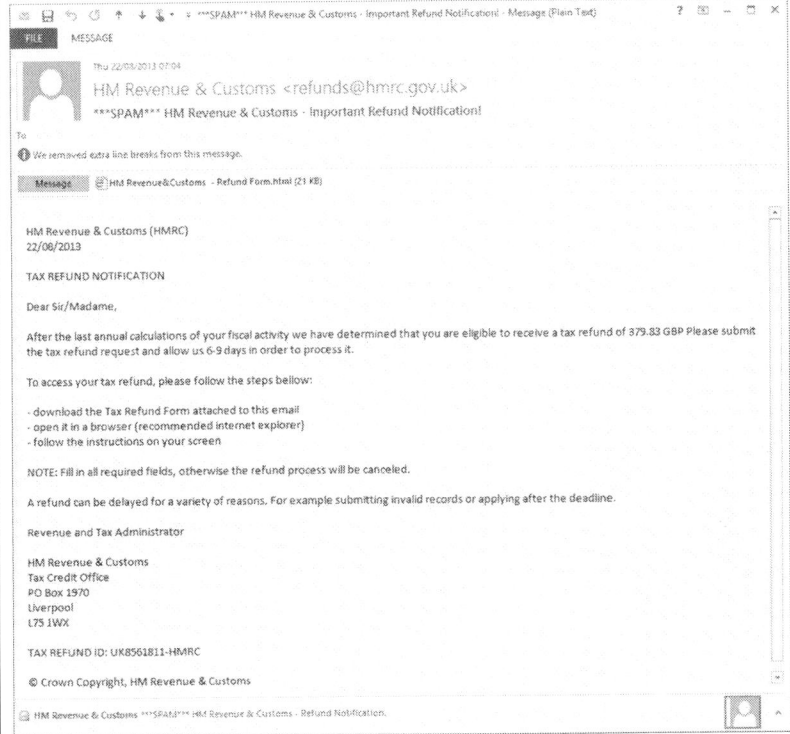

Ignore the whole ***SPAM*** bit, that's just cause my email filtering picked it up (I dug it out of my spam archive just to show you...)

Simply it 'looks' like an e-mail from HMRC telling you you've got a Tax Refund. You just need you to fill in the attached form for them to process it.

But it's not, as someone I came across recently found out, once you open up the attachment (**TIP:** NEVER open up HTML attachments unless you are **117% sure** they are legit, even if sent from someone you know... one of the easiest ways to get a virus).

The virus they got was particularly nasty, we ended up having to rebuild their machine for them as our conventional cleaning methods just wouldn't clean it up properly...

Maybe an accountant out there will tell me different, but I've never known HMRC to send an email about a refund, they always sent in the post (and usually asking for money, not giving it back!)

(On a side note, this email was a Blatant spam e-mail, aside from the look of it, there were several 'behind the scenes' tell tale signs that EVERY E-Mail filtering system should have picked up, if you got one of these and your e-mail filtering didn't pick it up, you need to get some better email filtering, because you are almost certainly at high risk of getting a virus... drop me a note if you want some help)

Top Tip

Always be suspicious of e-mails asking you to open up HTML attachments, they are a really easy way to send viruses.

If you are receiving a lot of these types of e-mails you really should talk to your IT people about your Anti-Spam, cause it should be blocking e-mails like this.

I'm thinking of setting up a free E-Mail checking service for people to send e-mails they are not too sure about over for us to check for them - Do you think that would be useful and **is it something you might use?**

```
From: Chris Blunt chrisblunt@busstopgroup.co.uk
Sent: 10th October
```
Subject: **I'm just trying to get home**

A really simple one for you this week, but done right it's going to make your life a whole lot easier and will be quicker to get stuff done on your computer...

I've often get asked the question, *Why does it take so long for the internet to start up?*

So, naturally, the first thing I do is open up their web browser *('the Internet', 'Internet Explorer','Google Chrome','FireFox','Safari' - you get the picture)...* and quite often what I find is they've got 6 or 7 Tabs set to open up straight away.

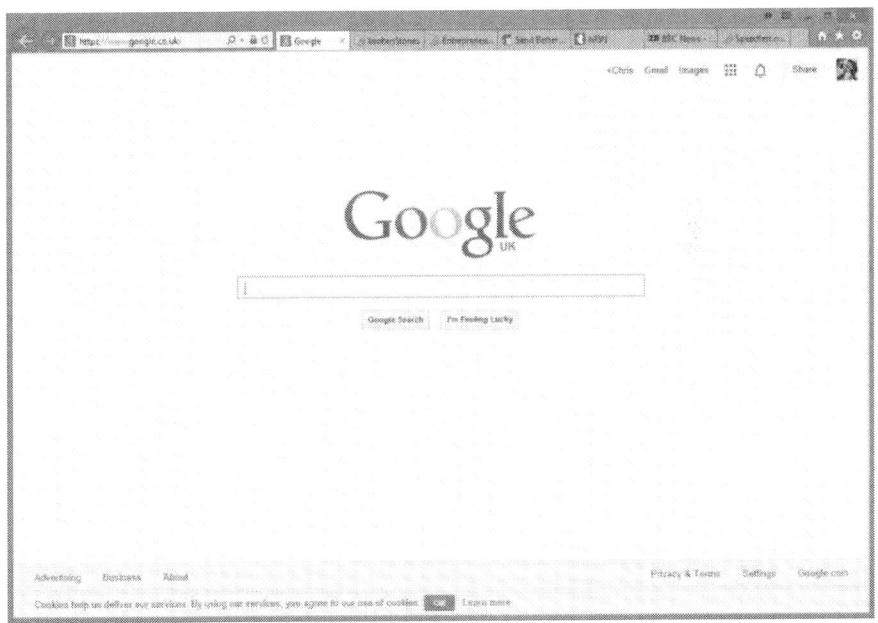

Each one of those tabs takes a little time to load, and more often than not I see people close half of them straight down! So what's the point in having them open up in the first place?

So just how do you set your home page then?

There are several ways to set your home page in each type of web browser. What I've done for you is put together a quick video of the simplest way for the top 3 browsers. My recommendation to you would be to set your home page to a very simple page (or blank), especially if you've got a slow internet connection.

Personally I have mine set to either a blank page, or the basic Google Search Page (Because that's most often where I need to go first!).

I've create 3 really short videos showing you how to change your Home Page in Internet Explorer, Google Chrome and Firefox.

How to Set your Home Page in Internet Explorer

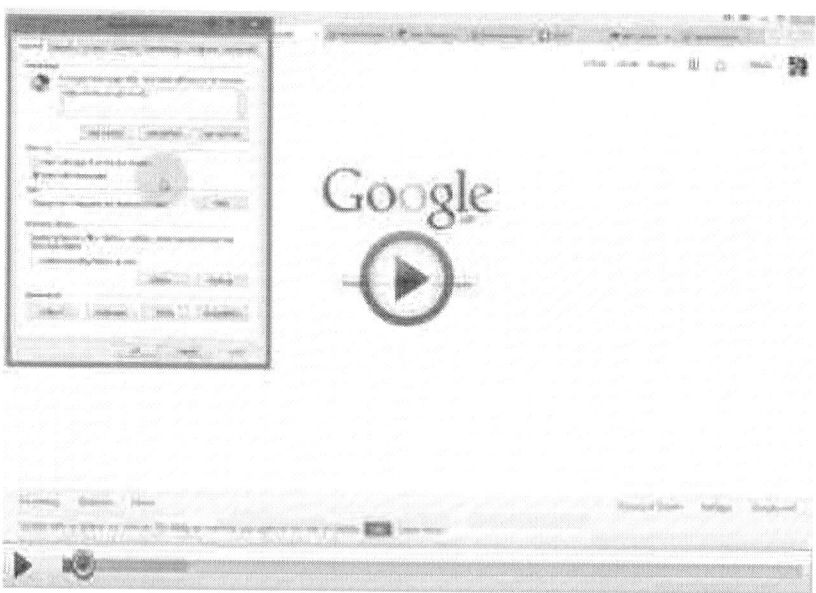

How to Set Your Home Page in Google Chrome

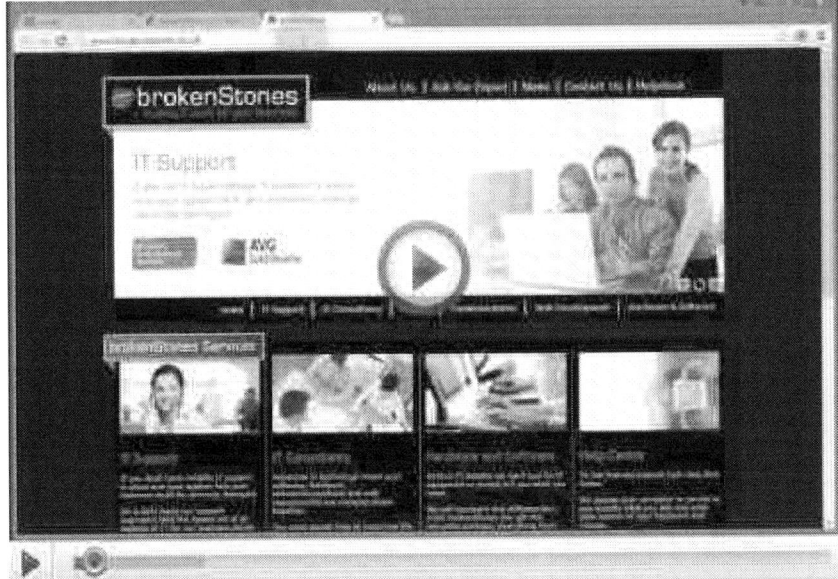

How to Change your home page in Firefox

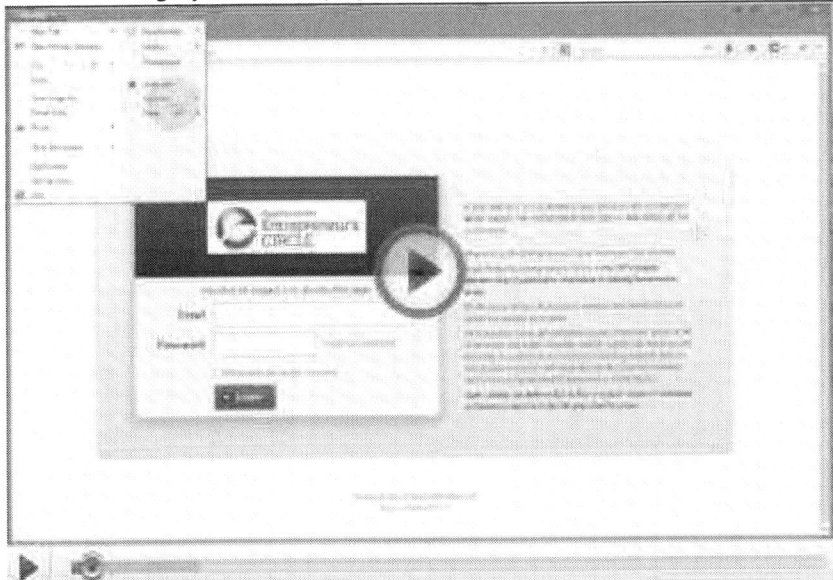

> **Giveaway #12 – How to Videos**
>
> The thing about a printed book, is you can't embed videos... so instead I've made them available for you here...
>
> http://chrisbluntbooks.co.uk/homepagevideos

Top Tip

If you are finding your web browser takes a long time to start up, check how many pages load when you first open it up, and try setting it to a blank page, or something really simple.

I have my Laptop set to a blank page, cause I never know what type of internet connection I'm going to be on and how slow it's going to be...

```
From: Chris Blunt  chrisblunt@busstopgroup.co.uk
Sent: 17th October
```
Subject: **Please see the attached**

I am forever sending and receiving documents attached to e-mails, and it amazes me how many people still send stuff through as word documents, and it's all messed up because they've either got a different version of word, or used some fancy fonts that I've not get.

And the worst thing of all, there is no need for that to happen... for over 6 years now Word has had the ability to 'Export to PDF' (and if you are using a version older than Word 2007,**Why?** you are missing out on LOADS of stuff and making your life more difficult... oh, and there is still a solution! ask me how...)

So when you've spent ages getting that word document to look just right, with the right fonts and the boxes all in the right place, you want the recipient to see it as you intended right?

Well if you are sending it through as a word document, there is a high chance they won't...

You see first of all Word tends to open up e-mail attachments in 'Protected View', and you need to click to open up normally... (have a look next time you get a word document as an attachment, if you got one of the latest version of word you'll notice it says 'Protected View' at the top).

Then if you get past that, you are then relying on someone having the same fonts that you've used, and if you've got some nicely laid out tables and boxes (as on a lot of quotes) then unless they've got the same version of word there's a good chance they'll all be muddled up...

So the EASY way to email a word document over to someone is as a

PDF.

How to Export as PDF in Word 2013

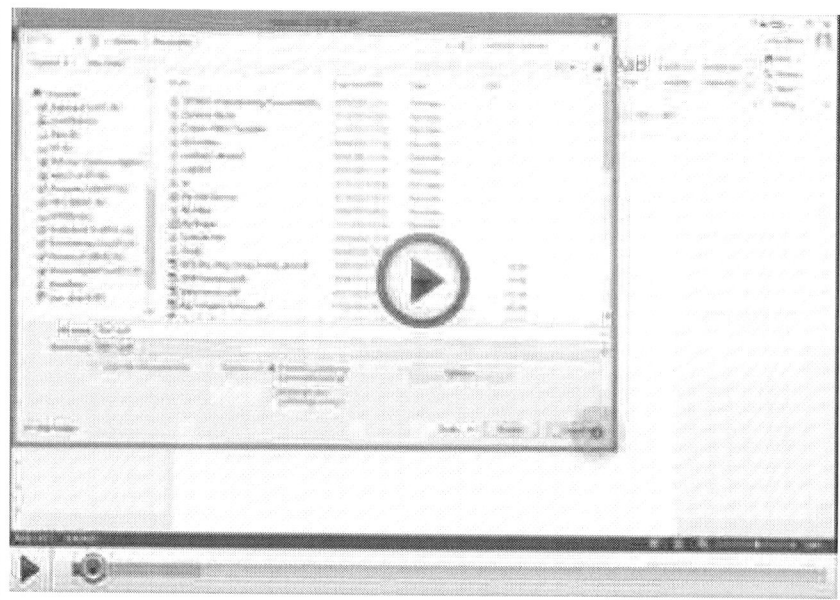

How to Export as PDF in Word 2010

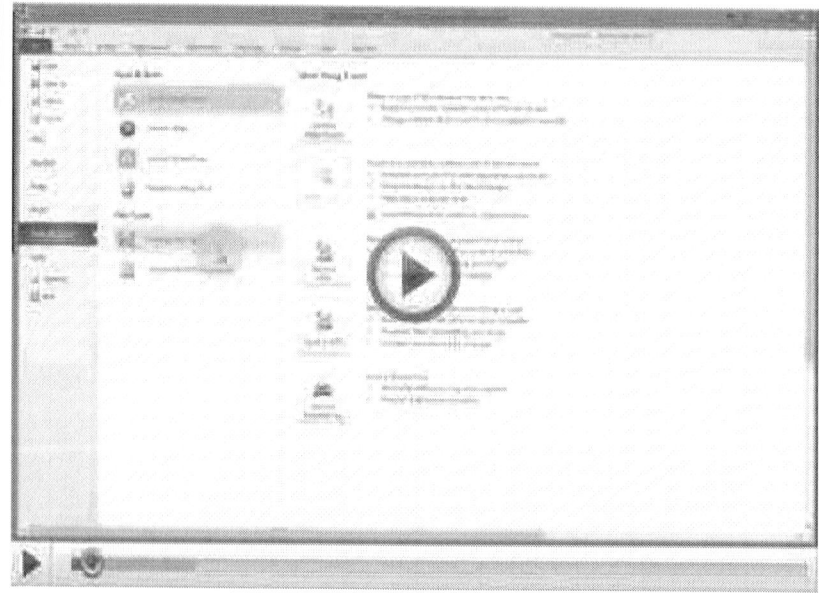

Top Tip

Unless you really want someone to be able to edit your document, it's best to send them through as PDFs, it's much easier to know that they'll see your document as you intend, and you don't have to worry about if they've got the right version of Word or not...

Giveaway #13 – How to Videos

Again displaying the videos in this book is somewhat tricky, so if you want to watch them jump over to

http://chrisbluntbooks.co.uk/word2pdf

From: Chris Blunt chrisblunt@busstopgroup.co.uk
Sent: 24th October
Subject: **Are you online?**

I've had quite a few people now ask me about being able to get reliable internet access when they're out and about, relying on other peoples WiFi connections is not always possible, and they're not always that great

Well the good news is **there's two great, really simple ways that I use to get online, and you can too.** They will cover yourself in almost all situations. One is super, 1 button press easy, and the other is almost as easy (it takes 3 button taps!).

I use both, and I've used them in all kinds of situations:

- whilst **sat in** hospital **waiting rooms** (especially useful earlier this year with all the endless appointments before my 2nd daughter arrived! literally hours of usage),
- **motorway service stations**, fixing someone's computer **in-between meetings**,
- in the **middle of the Welsh mountains**, doing my on-line banking...
- and of course whilst sat with a customer - I had **faster internet access in my pocket than they did in their office**!

The First **Super Easy, don't even have to think about it** way is to get yourself a **4G WIFI Dongle**, they are about £15/Month, and in my experience is they **work fantastically well (I get better signal on my 4G dongle than I do on my mobile phone!).** For me, needing always on, super fast internet access a complete no brainer... often it's **better than using your home or office internet!**

The Second, almost as easy way is to use the **personal hotspot**

on your mobile phone, I'm going to show you how to do that on the iPhone, but I know it's possible on several other phones (Just search for 'Tethering' and your phone model...)

Tethering basically uses your own mobile phone as a portable WiFi device, it uses you phones Data Connection (so relies on your phone having a signal! - That's why I carry two devices, on different networks!), and uses the data allowance you have as part of your phone contract...

Here how to set-up you Personal Hot Spot on the iPhone

Tap Settings, and you will see a 'Personal Hotspot' option (if you don't you might need to speak to your mobile provider about getting this enabled!)

On the Personal Hotspot screen, flick the switch to On, then make a note of your 'WiFi Password' (I've blurred mine out below, it'll be automatically generated for you). You can then Search for wireless networks on your Laptop or iPad (**It'll be called something like "Chris's iPhone"**)

Once it's turned on you'll get a bar across the top of your iPhone and tell you how many devices are connected. Always remember to turn it off when you're not using it, and remember it's using the data from your Mobile phone Plan. (I've got a 2GB allowance on my phone and never had a problem!)

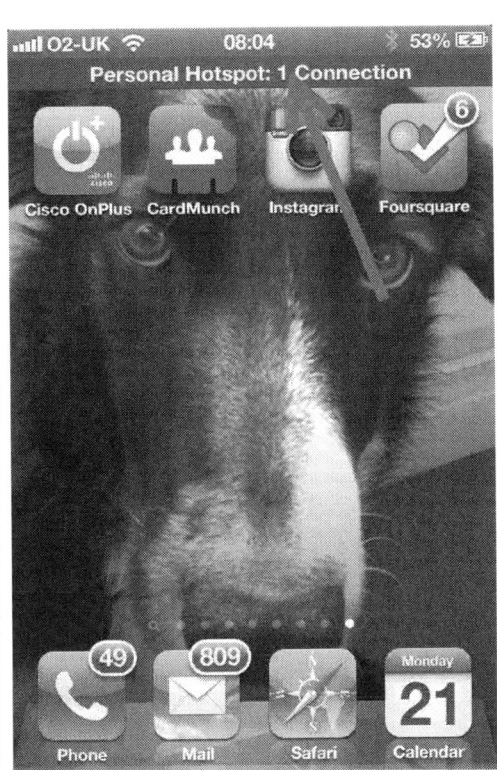

Top Tip

Getting a 4G Dongle and/or using the Hotspot on your phone is a great way to save faffing about with unreliable public (or private!) WiFi hotspots...

If internet access is important to your business, get yourself a 4G dongle and make sure you know how to use the personal hotspot on your phone..

Next week: I feel another RANT coming on, I've had enough of other IT bods putting windows 8 down, I'm going to tell you all why I believe **Windows 8 is the best operating system for business yet**, and how it's **helped me be more successful** in business. This is one NOT to be missed...

From: Chris Blunt chrisblunt@busstopgroup.co.uk
Sent: 31st October
Subject: **What is the problem?**

I'll make no apologies today, there has been a lot of misinformation and lies told by people who either can't be bothered to, or don't want to take the time to stop and think a little.

I am talking specifically about Windows 8 and others within the I.T. profession, and I figured it was time I spoke up about it, because they are doing you a disservice.

You see I have been personally using Windows 8 since late last year, and I love it! Sure it took a little while to adjust to it, but once you get used to it, and understand what Microsoft have done - and why - it's fantastic. **It does truly make my daily life easier and it's quicker to get stuff done.** And let's face it, that's what computers are for, to help us get more stuff done in less time.

The beef I have is when other I.T. Professionals - who you look to for advice and guidance - are giving out bad information. **Windows 8 is here to stay, I really believe it makes life easier, you've just got to understand one key concept...**

I spent a few minutes talking with Sarah the other week, she'd just got a new laptop with Windows 8 on it, and her usual I.T. person had told her how bad it was and had kindly installed a 'Start Menu' on there for her, so she could use it... trouble was she couldn't.**Sarah was still struggling with it**... that's how we got talking, After explaining the concept to her for a couple of minutes, then uninstalling the funny Start Menu thing the other guy had installed **I show her this trick,** and it started to make sense for her...

Here's the Trick
Microsoft saw that the start menu was central to your usage of the computer, it's the place you go to to access most of your programs... and what happens, after you'd had your computer a while and you've installed a few programs, is this... you click the start button, then you go to programs, then you scroll down a bit, then you click another folder, then you move the mouse over a bit, then just as you get to the program you want the mouse jumps, the menu disappears and you have to start all over again... Sound Familiar?

Well all Microsoft have done is **taken that start menu, and given it it's whole own screen**... yes, **everything on your start menu is now displayed across the entire screen**, making it dead easy for you to scroll and find what you are looking for... and it get's better... if you're reading this on windows 8 right now try this...

Press the start button on your keyboard (The windows Key), type *note* then hit enter... for those of you without windows 8, here's what happens...

Giveaway #14 – Windows 8 How To Video

I had a bit of a thing for Videos around this time (playing with my new software!) so you can view the Windows 8 Video here:

http://chrisbluntbooks.co.uk/win8video

113

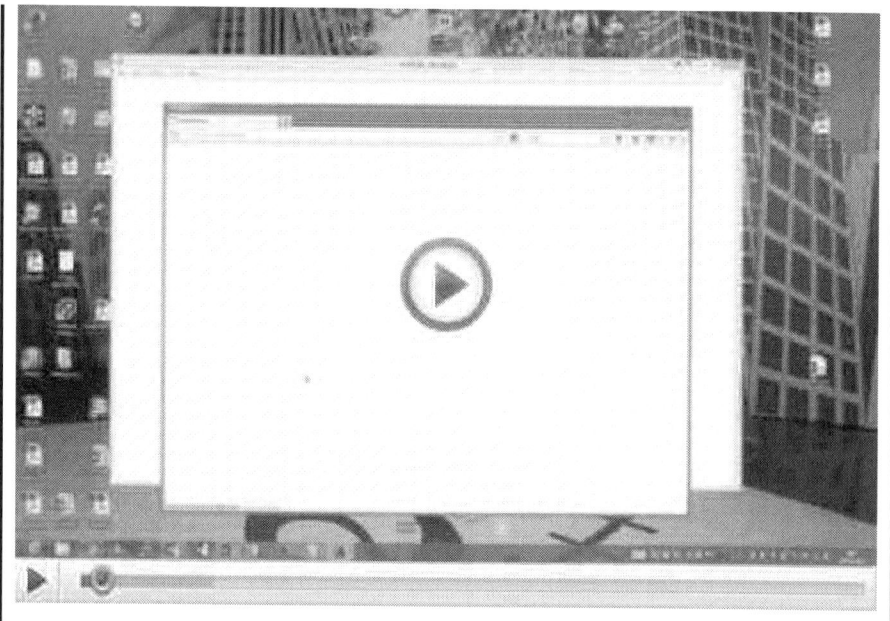

As you can see, I've opened both notepad and Firefox (I added Firefox in to prove a point, would have been a super short video otherwise!) in under 5 seconds, without taking my hands off the keyboard... just try and do that with a mouse and a start button?

Now bear in mind **you can do that with ANY program on your start menu** (or screen), how much time do you waste in a day clicking? That's just one of the reasons I love windows 8, it helps me get more stuff done!

Look if you've got 50+ computers and they are all running windows 7, then you're not really going to be thinking about upgrading yet, clearly that needs to be done in a structured and methodical way, but if you've only got one or two, and you've still got Windows XP (or the in-between one - Vista) then **you really need to be upgrading soon**, even if you've got 5 or 10 machines... If you're unsure talk to me...

Top Tip

Windows 8 really does **help me get more stuff done in less time**, if you've been holding back because all you've heard is bad things about it... don't, take it from someone who's been using it for the best part of a year, **it's one of the better ones, it's hear to stay, and it will make your life easier**...

Oh and if you're still on Windows XP, you REALLY need to be upgrading soon, did you know it's now over 12 years old? What Mobile Phone did you have 12 years ago? What Car did you have?

From: Chris Blunt chrisblunt@busstopgroup.co.uk
Sent: 7th November
Subject: **Simples**

The 2nd Most Hated thing about windows 8... and what to do about it...

This will take you 30 seconds at most to change, but it's probably the 2nd biggest moan I hear after 'There is no Start Button'.

Don't you hate it, when in windows 8 you open an image and it pops up in the stupid App Mode and takes you away from your desktop? and then it's a right faff to get back? You end up pressing start & escape 20 times before clicking madly and then your desktop magically re-appears?

Well you don't have to put up with that any more... here's the dead simple way to change it...

Find any image, right click on it, then choose 'properties'. In the window that pops up look for where it says "Opens With" and click the change button...

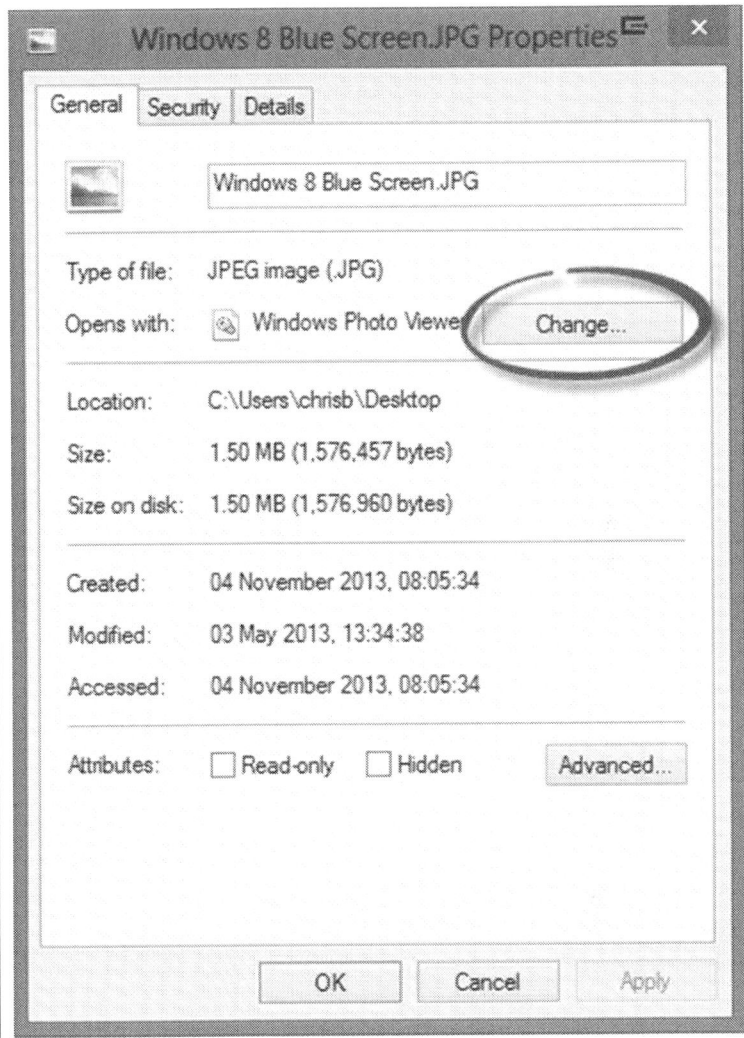

Then in the menu that pops up choose 'Windows Photo Viewer', Hit OK and it's all done.

Now when you double click that image you should find it opens up in the traditional windows photo viewer?

You might need to set this individually for the different types of images you've got (JPG, PNG etc...)

Here's a quick video showing you step by step how to change it...

Why do photos open in the silly windows 8 app mode?

Top Tip

If you're often frustrated when Images open up in that silly Windows 8 App mode, then change it! Just change the default program that opens images, the video above shows you how!

Giveaway #15 – Image Viewer

This is the last video of this book... I promise!

http://chrisbluntbooks.co.uk/openingimages

From: Chris Blunt chrisblunt@busstopgroup.co.uk
Sent: 14th November
Subject: **I thought you were away?**

I've got a really strange sense of Deja-vu here, so my apologies if I've already mentioned this before?

One of the common questions we get asked several times a month, is how do I set my Out of Office?

The answer depends on what type of E-Mail system you are using... Firstly if you are using Microsoft Exchange or Office 365 is dead easy, in outlook simply Click 'File' at the top, then you'll see 'Automatic Replies'

Exchange & Office 365 - via Outlook

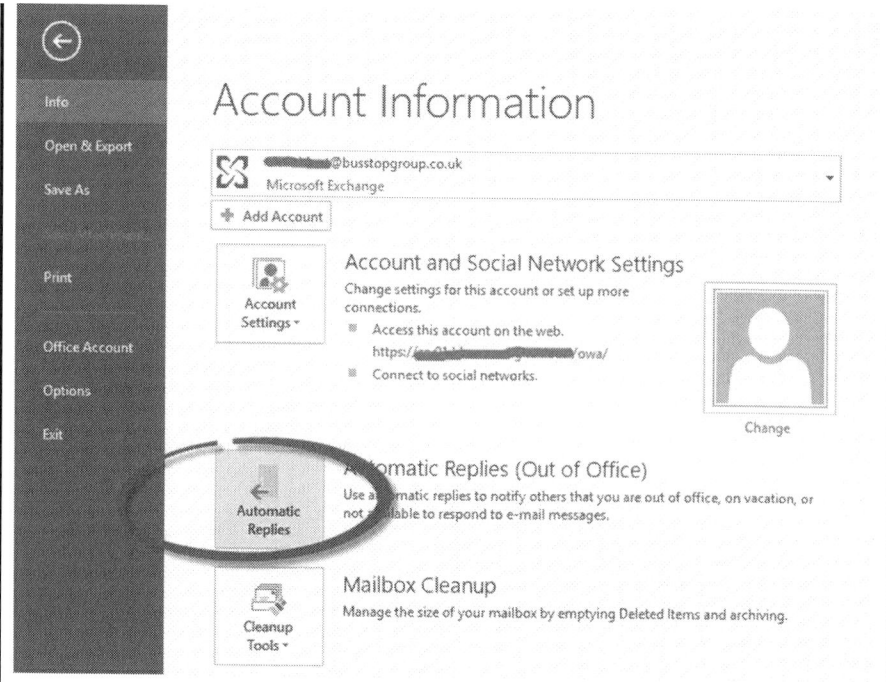

You will also notice now in outlook it tells you you've got Out of Office Set.

Or if you've not got outlook (or you are using Mac Mail) you can use the webmail option

Office 365 Webmail
Login to Office 365, Then click 'Outlook' on the menu bar at the top, then when you see your inbox click the cog in the top right

hand corner, then click 'Set Automatic Replies'

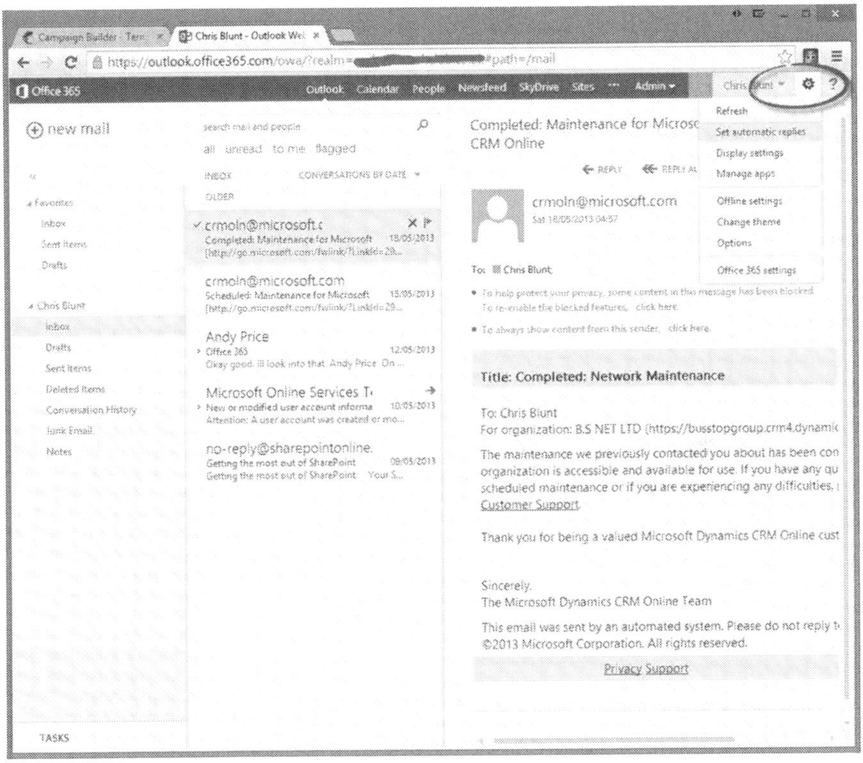

Microsoft Exchange Webmail

If you are used to using the Microsoft Exchange Webmail (AKA Outlook Web Access - or OWA) then just click the options button near the top right, then choose 'Tell People you're on Vacation'

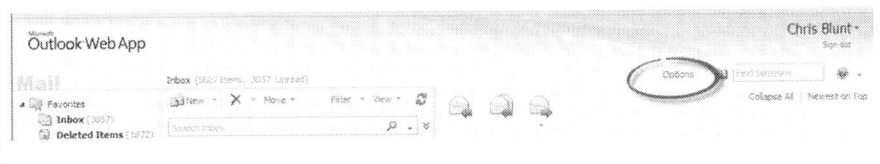

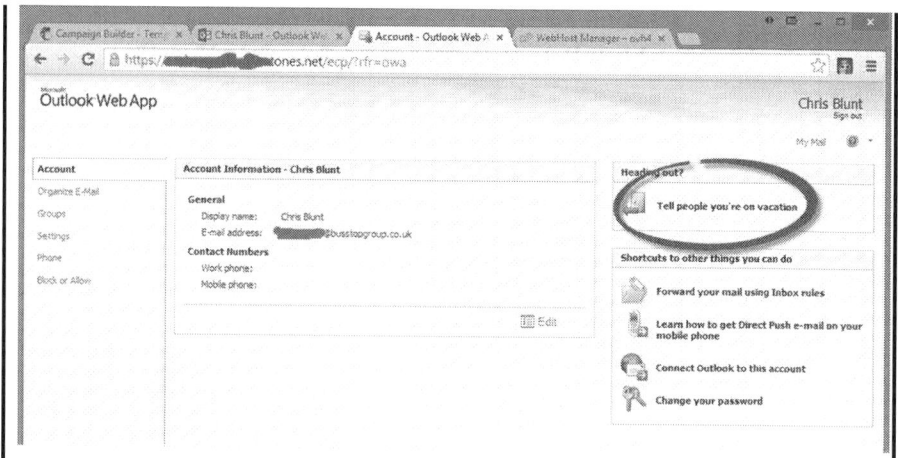

What if I'm not using Office 365 or Microsoft Exchange?

If you are using POP or IMAP or some other type of email system then how you set-up your out of office is dependant on how your e-mail provider has set their system up. It really does vary wildly (and sometimes not possible at all). A common method is via something called 'cPanel', login to your webmail (usually webmail.yourdomain.com if you're on cPanel) and then choose the 'Auto Responders' option - this is generally only available if your email host has allowed it...

As you know by now, I am really fond of Office 365, and here's another example if you are not already using it why it just makes things so easy... just saying!

Top Tip

Out of Office Replies are great for letting people know when you're not going to be about to answer your email, but also be a bit conscious about how often you put it on... I've seen some people use it to excess "I'm out for the next hour" type messages.

I tend to use mine when I'm away for several days and won't be checking email, and then sometimes when I'm back but have a lot to catch up on, so direct people to contact my support team for anything urgent...

From: Chris Blunt chrisblunt@busstopgroup.co.uk
Sent: 21st November
Subject: **One of the hidden costs in business**

To be honest with you, I have this conversation with a lot of people, but this one really shocked me, partly because we had the time to sit and write the numbers down, and when you look at the numbers they are pretty straight forward. (and yes sorry, I have got a bit mathematical with this one, but please bear with me)

We were talking about the cost of printing, they were complaining about how much they spend on ink each month, and how often they have to change the cartridges.

I had a bit of time so we started to write the numbers down…

- Cost of Printer - £50
- Pages Printed per Month 500 (That's one Pack of Paper)
- Cost of Ink Cartridges - £30
- Number of Pages per Ink Cartridge - 190 (at best, she felt like she was getting less)

So if you work that out, that's 6,000 pages a year, which is 32 Cartridges a year which is £960 on Ink per year!

Really? **£1,000 a year just on ink??**
That's about **16 pence for every page you print**…

So then we looked at what a decent printer would cost, and here's the thing, **it's paid for itself in under a year!**

For the package we looked at, a decent Low End HP Colour Laser

Printer / Scanner / Copier with a 3 year warranty and trimmings, with a years worth of toner it's about £750 all in...

After you've paid for the printer it's then going to cost you around **4.6 pence per page**, in this case the printer has well and truly **paid for itself in 8 months!** and you've brought your **ongoing costs down to around £270 a year**!!!

Here's another way to look at it, take the £1,000 budget you are going to spend on ink over the next year, spend around 3/4 that buying a new printer + toner, then take the other £250 and go and buy yourself something nice. Then next year take that same £1,000 budget, spend £270 on toner, then go spend £730 on something nice for you!

Is there anything to think about?

Top Tip

How much are you really paying for your printing? You can save yourself a bucket load of cash if you just make sure you get the right printer to your needs... It's a false economy to just go and buy any old cheap printer, you need to match the printer you get to the amount you print.
Next week: 3 Simple tricks to save you a bucket load of time...

Giveaway #16 – Print Cost Calculator

I've put together a handy print cost calculator to help you...

http://chrisbluntbooks.co.uk/printcostcalculator

From: Chris Blunt chrisblunt@busstopgroup.co.uk

Sent: 28st November

Subject: **Why is it some people can just do things quicker?**

I am going to get straight to the point today, computers are all about saving you time, and making it easier for you to get stuff done. Today I've got a little secret of how I get more stuff done on my computer...

Whenever anyone's sat next to me whilst I'm using my computer, one of the things they usually say is "How did you do that so quickly?"

It's easy, I use short-cut keys... rather than using the mouse (which requires hand eye co-ordination and is inherently slower - I'm sure some psychology books somewhere will tell you all about that if your interested...), I use the keyboard, you don't need to see what you are doing on the screen, just know what the short cut keys do and the computer will catch up with you.

I could write a book just on short cut keys alone, there is a key combination for pretty much everything you'd like to do... here's some of the shortcut keys I use every day,

My Top 5 Windows Shortcut Keys

Windows + E - Open up Windows Explorer (My Computer)

Windows + R - Open Up windows run Dialogue (I use this alot!)

Windows + L - Lock your computer, handy when you are stepping away

Windows + M - Minimize all your open windows - great when you need to find somethign on your desktop

Windows + Arrow Right - Snap your Current window to the right (Windows 7 & 8 Only)

My Top 5 Mac Shortcut Keys

Ctrl + Left / Right Arrow - Move Between Desktops

SHIFT + Command + I - When used in Safari will create a new e-mail with a link to the current page.

Command + Shift + D - Use in the finder Window to jump straight to your Desktop Folder

Option + Command + M - Minimize all your open windows.

Command + Shift + 4, Space Bar - Takes a Screen Shot of the current window

What's your Favourite Shortcut key?

Top Tip

It really pays to learn and get good at using short-cut keys, the more you can do without having to take your hands off the keyboard, the quick you'll get stuff done.

Bonus Short-cut Key
When writing an e-mail, rather than 'clicking send' when you're done, try pressing 'ALT + S' - that sends it for you... try combining that with Ctrl + N (New E-Mail) and you can write and send an email without going near the mouse!

```
From: Chris Blunt chrisblunt@busstopgroup.co.uk
Sent: 5th December
Subject: Don't jump off the bed!
```

There are only so many times you can tell someone something, in my daughters case, it was "don't jump off the bed". She's been told many, many times, and given the reasons why, but she still persists to do it.

This weekend though, she may have just learnt the hard way...

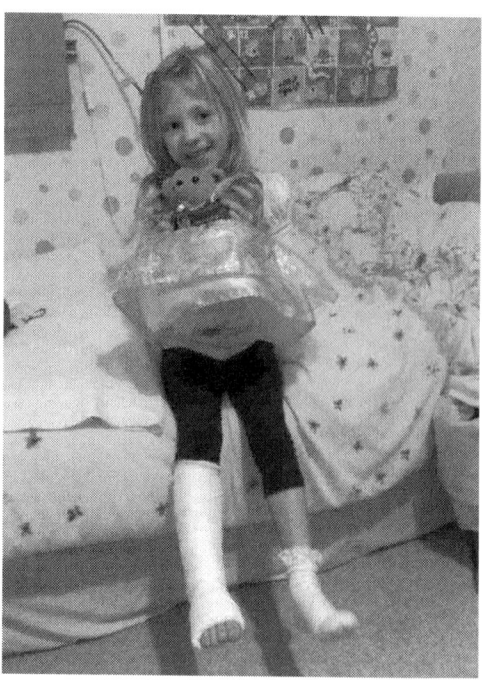

Ouch! She's broken her toe, the day before her 5th birthday party!

And this got me thinking how many times I tell businesses they REALLY need to make sure they've got good, reliable backups, because toe's heal, but if you lose some critical data it could be the end of your business. So here are my top 7 tips for good, reliable, secure backups...

| Don't learn YOUR lesson on backups the hard way!

Top Tip

Not one, but 7 today!

1. **Run Nightly backups as a minimum.** (a lot of stuff is now 'as it's changed')
2. **Verify your backups have run.** (more than once I've found people changing tapes, but the backup wasn't actually running!)
3. **Test your backups regularly.** (Do a test restore on a random file or document)
4. **Check you are adhering to Data Protection Laws.** (Where is it stored? Lookup the Data Protection Directive and EU Safe Harbour)
5. **Check your data is it stored sensibly.** (Where is it stored? Can you get it back quickly and easily if and when you need to?)
6. **Check you are backing up everything you need.** (Look at what are you backing up, have you included all your important files?)
7. Check software specific backup instructions. (Some Software - like sage - has its own backup routine to run, BEFORE you do your own data backup...)

From: Chris Blunt chrisblunt@busstopgroup.co.uk

Sent: 12th December

Subject: **What's Up?**

Here's a new one that has been doing the rounds lately, I've seen loads of these caught in our spam and virus filters.

As popularity has grown and more people have been using WhatsApp then it's been a good target for the scammers...

It's a really simple one, you'll get an email that looks very much like this..

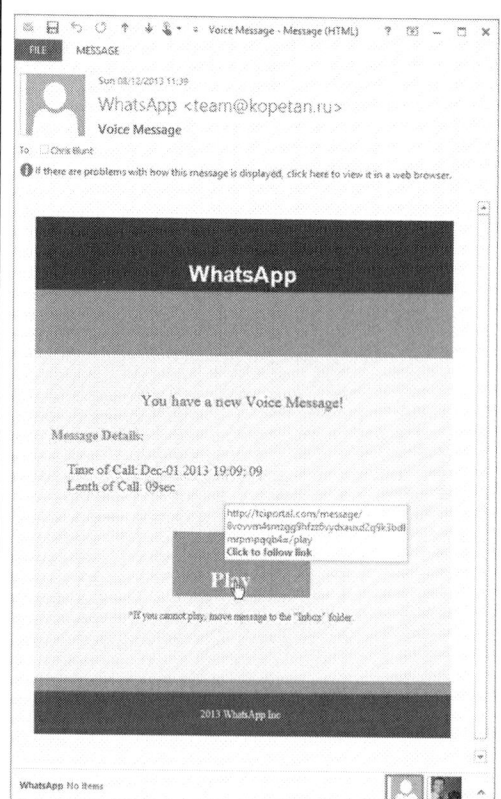

The short answer is, **if you don't use WhatsApp don't even think of clicking the play button** (Why would they send you messages when you don't use it?) and **if you do use WhatsApp, get your messages through the App itself**, not your email!

The almost as short answer is, **check out the 'From Address'** - it's a Russian domain, kopetan.ru, then **check out the link when you Hover** (don't click!) **over the play button**... both look **decidedly dodgy...**

Top Tip

I've said this many times before, but in the spirit of last weeks email...

If you are the tiniest bit unsure about and email **ALWAYS, ALWAYS, hover over any link's before clicking them!!** - I have seen it numerous times where a single click on the wrong website has destroyed someone's computer...

From: Chris Blunt chrisblunt@busstopgroup.co.uk

Sent: 19th December

Subject: **Can I get rid of all these cables?**

So this question has come up a several times in the last few weeks, but **thanks to Amy** for actually sending the question in.

"Should I upgrade our network to be all wireless?"

I've met several people who think that wireless is the way to go, and to **replace** their **wired** set-up **for** a **wireless** network.

The short answer is **Wireless is NOT a replacement for a wired network**, it's an enhancement to it.

A wired network can work at much, much higher speeds than a wireless one, which doesn't make that much difference if it's just you, your laptop and an internet connection. But if you're in an office, sharing data across other devices, it can make a massive difference.

Wireless is really handy, it means you can move around the office easily without having to worry where there's a spare network point or having to swap cables over, but with that convenience comes some sacrifices, a big one being speed and also reliability...

At this stage I could go all techno-babble on you, trying to explain the whys and wherefores, but chances are you're not going to read that, and I'm sure we've all got some last minute Christmas shopping to do!

So I'll keep it really simple.

Yes, it is good to implement wireless, but it's not as a replacement for Wired, purely an enhancement. You will get a **much better overall experience using a wired connection** (providing you're wired network has been set-up properly!)

Top Tip

If you are just jumping on the internet, or just working on some word or excel documents then wireless is fine, but if you are using something like Sage or working with large files you absolutely need to be on a wired network. There is no substitute.

From: Chris Blunt chrisblunt@busstopgroup.co.uk

Sent: 26th December

Subject: **Is this really what you want to read today?**

If you're reading this on the day I've sent it out, it's boxing day...

I could ask you why you are reading your emails today, but then you could ask me why I'm writing them?

So let's avoid that topic and instead I'll keep it really, really short.

Merry Christmas, Thank-you for reading my Top Tips in 2013, thank you to all of you that have sent in your feedback and questions over the last year.

If there are any burning issues you'd like me to cover in 2014 just drop me an email back,

I wish you all the success, happiness and Joy for 2014,

See you on the other side,

Chris.

Top Tip

One final tip for 2013, and it's a big one...

If you are still using Windows XP, you need to change it BEFORE April. It's a biggie!

From: Chris Blunt chrisblunt@busstopgroup.co.uk

Sent: 2nd January

Subject: **Reminder: Put the Bins Out**

It's the little changes than can make a big difference, and I did promise you another quick one this week...

So... **When did you last empty your bin**? And I'm not talking about the one in your office or Kitchen... but the one on your computer...

On the Mac it's called the 'Trash' and you should see an icon to the right side of the Dock at the bottom of your screen that looks a bit like this...

If you're using Windows it's often referred to as the 'Recycle Bin' and you should see it somewhere on your desktop looking like this...

Usually when you delete something on your computer it'll end up in the Recycle Bin / Trash just in-case you deleted it by accident,

135

But that's where it stays unless you go and empty it! We often find loads of old files in here, and it's one of the first things we do when running an MOT on someone's computer. It often frees up a big chunk of disk space and can sometimes help improve performance too (especially when you're low on disk space!)

Top Tip

Check and Empty your Recycle bin / Trash on a regular basis, it's just another thing that helps keep your computer healthy...

All you have to do is 'Right Click' on it and Choose Empty...

Giveaway #17 – Half Price MOT

As a thank you for reading this far in to my book have a half price Computer MOT... oh and if you are one of the first 20 people to claim it I'll pay for the other half for you!

http://chrisbluntbooks.co.uk/computerMOT

```
From: Chris Blunt chrisblunt@busstopgroup.co.uk
Sent: 9th January
Subject: Time for a change?
```

If there was one thing that could give anyone access to your entire life, how protective would you be of that thing?

Because in reality, for most people, your e-mail password is pretty close to doing that (once in to your email, most other stuff can be reset via email).

I read an interesting fact recently, **98.8% of all internet users share just 10,000 passwords**... that's a bit scary when you think there was 2.5 Billion internet users in June 2012...

So, **when did you last change your password?** and how secure is it?

If you have been reading since the start of Top Tips last February, you may remember "Chris's Tip's for creating a memorable, secure password"... you can grab it again here: http://chrisbluntbooks.co.uk/freepasswordguide.

Top Tip

'Cracking' your password is much easier than you might think, most dictionary words or names, even with numbers on the end, can be by passed in a matter of minutes.

Change your passwords frequently and create something a bit more secure.

> From: Chris Blunt chrisblunt@busstopgroup.co.uk
> Sent: 16th January
> Subject: **Can you use a different browser please?**

I can't believe I've not brought this up before, but are you using the wrong web browser?

At this point I have to save a big thank-you to 'J' for bringing this up - She asked to remain anonymous - though I don't know why it's a fantastic question!

Having **had trouble using a couple of websites** recently she was advised to try both Chrome and Firefox, and that prompted her to ask "What's the best browser to choose, and why does it matter that I use different ones?"

What's the best web browser to choose?
Short answer: All of them, and whichever one you feel most comfortable with!

Seriously, there is no right or wrong answer, you will get plenty of people tell you **'Oh you should be using Chrome, or Firefox'** but that's just their personal preference, use what you are used to using, that's **easiest for you to use.**

Why does it matter that I use different browsers?
The short answer is, it doesn't! Generally speaking The **Top browsers should all work pretty well with most of the websites out there.**

You will however get certain web applications that have been specifically built for a certain browser, and if a supplier recommends using a specific browser with their application then is it usually for good reason (most of the time!).

If you find a Web Application isn't doing what you think it should, try a different browser and see if that makes a difference.

What do I use?

Chrome, and **Internet Explorer**, and **Safari**, and **Firefox** (and and sometimes **Opera** - see below)

Up until recently I used to mainly use IE, which may surprise a few people, but generally I found it good to use, and was what I was used to. It was only because I had to do a substantial bit of work that required Chrome that I got used to using Chrome and have now switched.

I do however still use IE on a daily basis and Firefox gets fired up at least 2 or 3 times per week. Safari is the main browser on my Mac at home.

It's worth also mentioning an old favourite of mine, when I was travelling on the train a lot, and had slow & intermittent internet connection. I used to favour Opera, I was probably drawn in a bit by their slogan...

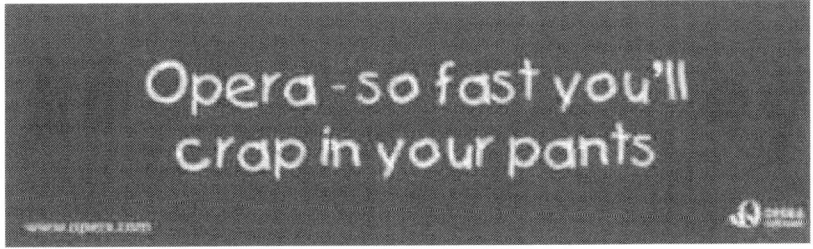

OK, that was just an excuse to get that image in there, but as far as strap lines go, it's a pretty powerful one (An no, there is no pun intended... I'll stop now...)

Top Tip

So there is no wrong or right answer as to which browser is the best. I'd recommended you have the 3 main ones all installed and ready to use if a particular site demands it, Chrome, Firefox & Internet Explorer (or Safari if you're mac based). Then use whichever one you feel most comfortable with day to day...

Hope that's helped and not just confused you more!

```
From: Chris Blunt chrisblunt@busstopgroup.co.uk
Sent: 23rd January
Subject: How did you do that?
```

Getting stuff done quicker then others is one of the things that gives you an advantage in life. It's something that people often comment on about me... **How did you do that**? how come your so quick?

Shortcuts has a lot to do with it. You see although a mouse makes it really easy to interact with your computer, it relies on **hand eye co-ordination** - you need to see what you are doing... and as any good magician will tell you, **the hand is quicker than the eye**, and it's harnessing the power of **keyboard shortcuts** that **can help you get stuff done quicker**.

One of the tools we use most on our computer has to be the web browser, So he's my **top 5 Browser shortcuts for getting stuff done quicker on the web**...

1 - New Tab
This one has to take the number one spot, it is probably my **most used keyboard shortcut** of all, it's a really quick way to open up a 2nd tab in your web browser,

Chrome / Internet Explorer / Firefox: CTRL + T
Safari: Command + T

2 - Open Link in New Tab
You know how when you search on Google and your not quite sure which search result might be what your looking for? Well hold down the Control Key and click all the ones you find

interesting... it'll open up that link in a **separate tab in the background**.. then you just need to go through them one by one rather than clicking back the whole time... (Works really well with the next one below!)

Chrome / Internet Explorer / Firefox: CTRL + Click Link
Safari: Command + Click Link

3 - Switch Between Tabs

I use this one a lot on my laptop, when I've got lots of tabs open, and it's a bit fiddly to get the touch pad in the right position (do you find it hard to use your touch-pad when your fingers are cold?). It's a quick and easy way to **cycle through your open tabs**, and **works well when you've got a lot of Google results to search through**...

Chrome / Internet Explorer / Firefox: CTRL + TAB
Safari: Command + SHIFT + [

4 - Find a Particular Word

If you are **searching for a particular item on a web page** this one comes in really handy, and saves you having to scan through loads of text for the right bit... Just hit CTRL + F to pop open a find box and then **type in the word or reference you are looking for**, then **hit enter to cycle through all the results**...

Chrome / Internet Explorer / Firefox: CTRL + F
Safari: Command + F

5 - See Recent Downloads

You know when you think you've downloaded something, but

can't find it? Just hit CTRL + J to pop open a window showing **your most recent downloads**, it's a **really quick and simple way to find that file you are looking for**...

Chrome / Internet Explorer / Firefox: CTRL + J
Safari: Option + Command + L

Top Tip

Learning to use Keyboard short cuts can dramatically increase the speed at which you use the computer. It may only be a few seconds each one saves you, but with hundreds to thousands of actions each day, it'll save you a bucket load of time!

Most stuff you do on the computer will have a keyboard short cut, think about what you do most, and try to find the short cut for it (Or let me know and see if I know one!)

```
From: Chris Blunt chrisblunt@busstopgroup.co.uk
Sent: 30th January
```
Subject: **Just forget about it**

One of the BIG problems I've been seeing lately is people having their **websites hacked**. Whether it's just something plain and obvious like your home page has been defaced or if it's a bit more sinister like your content has been changed or a **virus has been uploaded**.

Having your website hacked can have an impact in all sorts of ways on your business, from just **pure embarrassment**, to **lost sales** and in some cases **loss of email** or your entire **website** being **shut-down**.

It's a common misconception to think you can **just have your website built** and then **it'll look after itself**. That may have been true 10 years ago, but with the modern websites you need to be **keeping it maintained** with the **latest security updates**.

To be clear, **we don't create websites here**, but **we do host quite a lot of them**, and I see **daily attacks** on them. Most of them are **thwarted by the anti-hack software and procedures** we have in place, but **some sites are either too old**, or too **full of security holes** that it still keeps on happening, in those instances they have to roll back to a previous backup.

> **Top Tip**

So here's what you need to be checking:

Do you have a recent backup of your website? - Your Hosting Provider and / or your Web Developer should be able to help with this, check with them. Ideally you want nightly and/or weekly backups, or as often as your website changes...

Does your website have the latest security updates applied? If it's a WordPress Site there is usually a really handy 'Update now' button on your admin dashboard, but always a good idea to check with your web guy first in-case it breaks something!

Does your web host use Anti-Hack and Anti-Malware protection? This will help protect your site from common attacks and is a big help if you're not great at applying the latest security updates as soon as they are released.

Finally, **if your website is important to your business, it's really worth considering some kind of regular monthly maintenance package from your web developer**, most of them will offer them and look after all of the updates and security patching for you... just ask them!

From: Chris Blunt chrisblunt@busstopgroup.co.uk
Sent: 6th February
Subject: **I just can't do without two...**

As any addict will no doubt tell you, **One is never enough**... and for me this applies just as much to computer screens...

One of my cannot do with-out's is **two computer screens**, just to be clear this is two computer screens on one computer, both showing different things...

If you've not tried it, you really, really should... a bit like a mobile phone, **you'll wonder how you ever coped without** two once you've used them...

Why are they so useful?
They just enable you to be **so much more productive**... do you remember the old document holders? Where you'd have a handwritten note on a stand next to you monitor to reference? Well this is kind of like the next step up... having the ability to reference a web page on one screen whilst composing a document on the other. Sure you could switch between the two programs on one screen, but how much time and effort do you waste in doing that?

Two screens to me is all about getting more stuff done in a shorter time. You could argue it's not 'essential' to daily life, but it's things like this that make my life that bit easier using the computer, and help me get more done in less time than others.

There is absolutely no question about it for me, I know with all the time and effort it saves me, the small additional cost of a 2nd screen pays back easily within a month

Whether it's referencing facts, figures & prices on the left screen, whilst I compose my quote or proposal on the right, or writing an email reply on the right screen whilst referencing their original email on the left... I've even been known to watch a webinar on the left screen whilst I'm getting on with some routine work on the other

Last week I had a large diagram of someone's network and IT Infrastructure on the left screen, whilst I critiqued it and suggested improvements in word on the right. Had I not had two screens I'd have had to print out several pages, Sellotape them together and stick it on the wall... that would have driven me crazy and taken so much more time and effort...

For the record, I've tried 3 screens, side by side, but I didn't get on with them too well, it felt a bit like information overload,

Top Tip

Dual Screens gives you a distinct advantage in the battle to get more done in less time. If you've not tried it you are missing out.

If your desktop doesn't already support two screens you can usually easily get a 2nd graphics card for your computer, and you don't have to go for the super duper 24" ultra monitors I use either. You can get a decent 2nd monitor for less than £100 if you want. How many hours work would you need to save yourself to make that a worthwhile investment?

From: Chris Blunt chrisblunt@busstopgroup.co.uk

Sent: 13th February

Subject: **Are you happy to risk EVERYTHING?**

I've been through this many, many times, but there are still people out there risking everything... are you one of them?

I know I cover this topic a lot, but the truth is it's probably the **single biggest issue out there**, and although I should be used to it, it still shocks and worries me, and **you should be worried** too.

You see most people know they need to do backups, and a lot of people do actually have them set-up, but what let's a lot of people down is failure to check them.

Like the new customer I went to see last week, they had their **backups set-up**, they even had a whole stack of removable drives that they **changed every night**, but all of that was **completely useless**, because on the 13th of December last year someone had put their scheduled **backup job on Pause**!

Now their old IT company was supposed to have been checking these for them, but that's no excuse, it's **your data**, **your business at risk**, and ultimately **your responsibility**.

Maybe you don't have a legal responsibility to keep 7 years worth of records, but how would you feel if you lost everything over night?

Would you recover?

> **Top Tip**

I think the message is pretty clear this week,

Go and Check your backups NOW.

Test restoring a file, or ask your IT provider to restore a file for you... Trust me, you'll be glad you did.

From: Chris Blunt chrisblunt@busstopgroup.co.uk
Sent: 20th February
Subject: **An Intriguing Offer**

I've got some sad news for you... that was the last Top I.T. tip of this book...

The good news is the next one is well underway, and I'd love to feature you in it...

You've read all my book, you've seen the kind of questions people send me and the kinds of topics I cover... so why not send me your own question you'd like answered

So here is my intriguing offer to you... **Win a Free iPad**

and... **Win a Signed Copy of my Next Book**

I'm well underway with the next 52 e-mails and I'd love to feature you in the next book

---

The BIG Giveaway – Win a Free iPad!!

Send me your own question you'd like answering and you'll enter the draw to win a Free iPad...

http://chrisbluntbooks.co.uk/freeipad

Plus, if your question is relevant enough and it get's featured in the next book, you'll get a free Signed copy of the next book with my compliments too...

If you can't think of a relevant question to ask, don't worry, just send me some feedback on what you thought of this book and you'll also get entered in the iPad draw...

From: Chris Blunt chrisblunt@busstopgroup.co.uk

Sent: 27th February

Subject: **Want to know more?**

If you've found this book, and the tips in it useful, and you'd like to know more then you can signup to my weekly top tips right here: http://chrisbluntbooks/toptips/

If you want to get in touch with me, you can reach out to me via the following ways:

Blog:

http://letsbebluntaboutit.co.uk

Website:

http://brokenstones.co.uk

http://chrisbluntbooks.co.uk

http://busstopgroup.co.uk

Twitter:

@brokestones

@ChrisAndDonald

Facebook:

http://facebook.com/brokenstonesIT

LinkedIn:

http://uk.linkedin.com/in/chrisblunt/

brokenStones Helpdesk: (For all IT Support Enquiries)

01543 241 016

Amazon: Did you enjoy this book? If so please think about leaving me a favourable review on Amazon.

From: Chris Blunt chrisblunt@busstopgroup.co.uk
Sent: 06th March
Subject: **The Giveaways**

Throughout this book you'll have seen the 'Giveaway' boxes, I've listed them all here in brief for your convenience. In addition if you want the whole list emailed through to you just go to **http://chrisbluntbooks.co.uk/giveaways** and I'll send you a quick and easy reference to them all...

1. **Password PDF guide** - http://chrisbluntbooks.co.uk/freepasswordguide/
2. **Basic SPF Check** - http://chrisbluntbooks.co.uk/freeSPFCheck
3. **Video Tips** - http://chrisbluntbooks.co.uk/freeVideoTips
4. **Office 365 Free Trial** - http://chrisbluntbooks.co.uk/free365trial
5. **Free MAV Trial** - http://chrisbluntbooks.co.uk/freeMAVtrial
6. **Professional E-Mail** - http://chrisbluntbooks.co.uk/properEmail
7. **IT Clinic Ticket** - http://chrisbluntbooks.co.uk/itclinic
8. **Ask a Question** - http://chrisbluntbooks.co.uk/askaquestion
9. **Drop Box Link** - http://chrisbluntbooks.co.uk/dropbox
10. **E-Mail Signature Guide** - http://chrisbluntbooks.co.uk/signature
11. **Whois Lookup** - http://chrisbluntbooks.co.uk/whois
12. **Home Page How to Videos** - http://chrisbluntbooks.co.uk/homepagevideos
13. **Word Videos** - http://chrisbluntbooks.co.uk/word2pdf
14. **Windows 8 Video** - http://chrisbluntbooks.co.uk/win8video
15. **Change Image Viewer Video** - http://chrisbluntbooks.co.uk/openingimages
16. **Print Cost Calculator** - http://chrisbluntbooks.co.uk/printcostcalculator
17. **Computer MOT** - http://chrisbluntbooks.co.uk/computerMOT
18. **Win an iPad** - http://chrisbluntbooks.co.uk/freeipad

Top Tip

One Final Top Tip from me.

Please, Please, Please... if you find even just one page in this book useful..
RIP IT OUT!! Stick it on your wall... and use it...

Books are made to be used... not to sit on a shelf and get dusty...

Legal Disclaimer: I accept no liability or responsibility if you are foolish enough to try and rip a page out of your Kindle and stick that on the wall. Some Common Sense is required on your part before heeding this, or any of my advice!